Right Here...
Right Now...
Meanderings

By Diana Newquist Parson

Published by KDP Publishing
ISBN: 9798377937845
Copyright @2023

Dedicated

Right Here…Right Now…Meanderings is dedicated to my husband, Perry, who loves me unconditionally and encourages me to write.

It is also dedicated to my parents: Kenneth and Violet Mae Newquist. My parents encouraged me to observe, to write, to think, and to learn. My mother wrote down the stories and poems that I told her, even before I learned how to print.

And it is dedicated to Luke, Maddi, Bradden, Dylan, Zayden, Delilah, Darrell, Sherelyn, Shirley.

Finally… and over all and through all … it is dedicated to the glory of God.

Forward

This is the struggle: to be in the world but not of the world. We are surrounded on every side by the secular; yet as a believer in Jesus, I want to walk spiritually.

But the truth is that there is a sudden twist... a bend in the path... something catches my eye.... and suddenly I am meandering along the life trail. How do I keep the balance of walking in the world, yet focusing on the spiritual?

This book is a collection of original poetry and prose that catches me at various turns in the journey. The majority are not faith-filled. But they serve as a springboard to ponder faith-filled concepts. That's how I keep balance: using the world around me to remind me of Scripture and to remind me to pray.

Each poem and story is followed by Scripture, journaling and thought prompts, and prayer. Come... meander with me as we explore life, both physical and Scriptural.

Poetry

Prose

1. When She Plays Her Flute

When she plays her flute,
Kites fly,
Japanese kites,
Delicate dragons
With lacy fire breath.

When she plays her flute,
Snows fall,
Wandering snows
Dancing in spirals,
Teasing the wind.

When she plays her flute,
Crickets sing,
Mendelssohn crickets,
Hailing spring,
Lauding summer.

All this,
Tickling my fingers,
Sauntering and lullabying,
When she plays her flute.

======================================

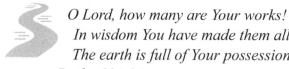

O Lord, how many are Your works!
In wisdom You have made them all;
The earth is full of Your possessions.
Psalm 104:24

You are the Lord, You alone. You have made heaven, the
heaven of heavens, with all their host, the earth and all
that is on it, the seas and all that is in them.
Nehemiah 9:6

In His hand are the depths of the earth; the heights of the
mountains are His also. The sea is His, for He made it,
and His hands formed the dry land.
Psalm 95:4-5

Meanderings: What parts of creation
move you to praise? What music helps
you reflect on God's glorious world?

Father, the beauty of Your creation stuns my mind!
Wherever I travel, the beauty unfolds: beauty of the sky,
the earth, the waters, the flowers and trees, the many
animals. It reflects Your glory, Your majesty. And I
thank You for the gift of music in this world. What I
hear... what I see... brings You honor. Help me
continue to know You through Your creation.

To God be the glory

2. Vacant

Her expression was vacant…
Like a house where no one lives any more.
Only the wind fills its corners,
Whistles at the windows,
Shakes the shutters
And knocks at the door.

===

 Come to Me, all who labor and are heavy
laden, and I will give you rest.
Matthew 11:28

Beloved, I pray that all may go well with you and
that you may be in good health, as it goes well with your
soul.
3 John 1:2

When the unclean spirit has gone out of a person, it
passes through waterless places seeking rest, and finding
none it says, 'I will return to my house from which I
came.
Luke 11:24

Meanderings: So many in our world
are trapped within mental and
emotional illnesses. Many are trapped

in dementia. How do you react to one like this? How can you show the love of God to an individual who suffers from this illness?

Father, help me be more aware of those who are bound in mental and emotional illnesses. Help me be sensitive to their needs, to try to understand their world. I thank You that You continue to love us even in the depth of the illness that threatens to overcome life itself. Help me show them Your rest.

To God be the glory

3. Has Anyone Seen My Glass Slipper?

There's something about a room
Cigar- stinky with carelessly tossed coats,
A poet in residence,
And Sartre at midnight
That makes me want
To catch a pumpkin going my way
And crawl into familiar ashes.

(Winner of *Writer's Digest* Creative Writing Contest, Poetry, 1978)

==

 Save me, Lord,
*   from lying lips*
*   and from deceitful tongues.*
Psalm 120:2

Don't love this evil world or the things in it. If you love the world, you do not have the love of the Father in you. 1 John 2:15

Meandering: What are some worldly situations that tend to draw you? How do you resist? What are the familiar ashes in your life?

Father, When I am where You do not want me to be, I pray that You will help me find the way home. You are home! You are where I want to be. Help me renounce worldly pleasures, and look for what You are doing in this world.

To God be the glory

4. Ask Her Name

Did I show you my picture?
Forgive me if I already showed you.
It's all I have and I can never take another.

Her little smile…
it will always be that way.
And her clear blue eyes….
They used to look up at me,
But now look at Jesus.

Let me show you my picture.
Go ahead.
Ask her name.
I'm glad to tell you.

(Dedicated to Lisa Blossom Payne, in memory of Mari)

===

 Truly my soul finds rest in God;
my salvation comes from Him.
Psalm 62:1

And the testimony is this, that God has given us eternal life, and this life is in His Son.
1 John 5:11

Meandering: Has there been a death that affected you greatly? Why is it important that others not forget his or her name? How did you seek the Lord during that time?

Father, We need You. When in sorrow, we need Your perfect rest. I can trust Your Word... Please... Just help me rest in You. Help me remember that You provided eternal life through Jesus.

To God be the glory

5. Milady

Tread easy, now.
The world's slowing down.
Here comes Milady
In her rustling gown.
And colors? What colors!
All gold and brown.
She's stepping softly
On dying ground.

Goodby to her sister,
Hello to her brother.
Soon she'll be gone,
Then another... And other.

Walk carefully, now.
Milady draws near
To whisper her charms
In my gullible ear.

(Published in *Synapse*, 1969)

===

 *While the earth remains, seedtime and harvest,
cold and heat, summer and winter, day and
night, shall not cease.*
Genesis 8:22

*He changes times and seasons; He removes kings and
sets up kings; He gives wisdom to the wise and
knowledge to those who have understanding
Daniel 2:21*

Meanderings: Can you find God in
the changing of the seasons? Which
season shows God most to you?

*Father, All praise for how You designed our world, with
the changing of the seasons that reminds us of You.
What wonderful colors You made! Help me remember
that You are in charge, that You control the times and
seasons, that Your ways are perfect and always on time.*

To God be the glory

6. Dig Me a Hill

"Dig me a hill."
I smiled at her prattle.
For how could her innocence
Know of impossible?
How could her childishness
Delve physical truth?

"Dig me a hill."
To amuse her, I spaded.
Finished, I said, "See, it's a hole."

She laughed in awareness.
"Ah, but the heap close beside is a hill!"

(Dedicated to Shirley Newquist Reid)

(Published in *Synapse*, 1969)

==

 And looking at them Jesus said to them, "With people this is impossible, but with God all things are possible."
Matthew 19:26

Truly, I say to you, whoever does not receive the kingdom of God like a child shall not enter it."
Luke 18:17

But Jesus said, "Let the little children come to Me and do not hinder them, for to such belongs the kingdom of heaven."
Matthew 19:14

Meanderings: Has a child ever taught you a lesson? How does a child's simplicity affect the lesson or truth?

Father, Help me come to You as a child, who believes that the impossible is possible. Help me to learn and grow into such a belief of You.

To God be the glory

7. Gershwin Summer

White Gatsby sun
Shimmies on the highway
While Queen Anne's lace
Jitters in the wind
To faint frog jazz.

===

Shout for joy to the LORD, all the earth, burst into jubilant song with music; make music to the LORD with the harp, with the harp and the sound of singing, with trumpets and the blast of the ram's horn— shout for joy before the LORD, the King.   Let the sea resound, and everything in it, the world, and all who live in it
Psalm 98: 4-7

Let the heavens rejoice, let the earth be glad; let the sea resound, and all that is in it.   Let the fields be jubilant, and everything in them; let all the trees of the forest sing for joy.
Psalm 96: 11-12

Meanderings: What songs give you joy? What is a favorite song to lift your spirits? Have you ever spontaneously burst into song?

Father, I so love music. Music that praises You. Music that helps me remember. Music that makes my feet tap and my hands clap. Music that heals my heart and wipes my tears. To sing! To make music! To listen to the world around me create song! Thank You for music!

To God be the glory

8. New Shoes

When I smell stiff leather of new shoes,
It is 1955 and Bill Haley and the Comets rock
From the car radios outside the shoe store.
Inside is cool, dim, proper, with
Suited salesmen carrying metal foot measurers and
Squatting before me with boxed samples.

I step onto the foot X-ray machine,
Push the button,
Watch my toe bones squiggle,
Marveling at seeing my insides as well as my outside.

My heart wants a pink pair of sandals
With glitter on the straps,
Just right for dancing the night away,
And my mother nodding no, no,
Bring her a pair of sensible oxfords.

Now my daughter and I enter the shoe store at the mall.
Pounding music beats my headache
While tattooed young things wander the aisles.
We, too, wander, searching carelessly stacked boxes.

She wants the boots with chunky soles, thick laces.
I see her in pink sandals with glitter.

Where is the machine that will let me see her insides
As well as her outside?

==

Your kingdom is an everlasting kingdom,
And Your dominion endures throughout all
generations.
Psalm 145:13

How great are His signs
And how mighty are His wonders!
His kingdom is an everlasting kingdom
And His dominion is from generation to generation.
Daniel 4:3

Now to Him who is able to do far more abundantly
beyond all that we ask or think, according to the power
that works within us, to Him be the glory in the church
and in Christ Jesus to all generations forever and ever.
Amen.
Ephesians 3:20-21

Meanderings: What do you fear for the next generation? How can you pass on the good news of God's love and salvation to those who come after you?

Father, help me to not be dismayed at differences in generations. Rather, please help me to embrace the new generations, just as the older generations embraced me. Help me remember that embracing does not mean to give permission to do anything, but rather that we teach the younger generations of You! Help me pass on Your love, Your teaching, Your Word. May this next generation see You for Who You are.

To God be the glory

9. Buffalo Ranch Out Longmont Way

Walking rails tangled in brier,
Hot from 3:00 Colorado sun,
Playing train, messing around,
'til Ed put up his hand
To gesture quiet
'cause round the bend it began
To be full with buffalo.

Two bulls nudged a line in dust;
A cow licked her calf.
Three or four rolled in the wallow,
And balding old ones
Dozed in the sun.

We hid behind the gooseberries,
Watching them play
In sunshine.

Buffalos.
And us.
And sunshine.

===

 From the rising of the sun to the place where it
sets, the name of the LORD is to be praised
Psalm 113:3

Then God said, "Let Us make man in Our image, after Our likeness. And let them have dominion over the fish of the sea and over the birds of the heavens and over the livestock and over all the earth and over every creeping thing that creeps on the earth."
Genesis 1:26

Meandering: What experience has helped you to appreciate God's creation? What was a "wow" moment?

Father, All praise to You for Your creation, for the sunshine, for Your provision. Help me be a good steward of your creation, using plants and animals wisely. Make me ever aware of Your presence in Your creation.

To God be the glory

10. Master Designer

Pastel bodies
In search of an artist
Lie about the palette,
Waiting for a brush
To form a portrait
With a crimson soul.

==

For You created my inmost being;
You knit me together in my mother's womb.
I praise You because I am fearfully and
wonderfully made; Your works are wonderful,
I know that full well.
Psalm 139:13-14

So God created man in His own image, in the image of
God He created him; male and female He created them.
Genesis 1:27

Meandering: How can you be a
crimson soul in a pastel world? What
kinds of color can you share with your
world?

Father, We praise You for creating us... For giving us body and soul... For life itself. Help us to be the vibrant color for You in this world. Help me remember that Your creation of man and woman was perfect, and in Your own image. What honor!

To God be the glory

11. This Was My Room

"This was my room,"
And I welcomed you over
The splintered thresh
Into that dusky place
Of yesterday.

"The bed was here, my chair,
The mirror… Here.

The walls were white,
The spread deep blue.

I dreamed here of you
Before I met you,
Before I knew your name.

And I knew, Dear,
That someday
You would come with me
To trace your initials
On my window."

(Dedicated to my husband, Perry Parson)

===

I wait for the Lord, my whole being waits,
and in His word I put my hope.
Psalm 130:5

Wait for the Lord;
Be strong and let your heart take courage;
Yes, wait for the Lord.
Psalm 27:14

Meandering: How is waiting on the Lord difficult? How have you experienced waiting on the Lord? What has been a benefit of waiting on God's plan?

Father, I thank You for helping me wait for just the right husband. Thank You for protecting me from the mistakes I could have made so easily. I praise You for bringing my husband to me, and for our years together.

To God be the glory

12. Legacy in a Cinnamon Can

Cached in a niche,
A tin of treasures
Hoarded by busy hands
In hours long forgotten.

Two marbles
("Betcha one cat eye 'gainst two aggies")
An ivory sliver,
("Fairy left 50 cents")
A golden strand tied in pink,
Faded flowers, tiny beads,
Quaint papers from another age.

Sweet spice gesture
In that old cinnamon can,
A promise to endow long ago tomorrows
With wealth of today.

==

*Better is a little with the fear of the Lord
than great treasure and turmoil with it.
Proverbs 15:16*

Praise the LORD. I will extol the LORD with all my
heart in the council of the upright and in the assembly.
Great are the works of the LORD; they are pondered by
all who delight in them.
Psalm 111:1-2

Meanderings: What brings back
memories for you? How are those
memories treasures? How does God
speak to you though memories?

Father, Thank You for the treasure of memory: for the
little trinkets, the humble word that brings the memory
to mind. In Your wisdom, You have not blessed me with
great wealth, but You have given me the treasure that I
desire: Jesus, eternal life, and memories. Help me
ponder on what You have given me.

To God be the glory

13. Spring Imp

Listen!
Do you hear it?
It's the spring imp, loose again.
And his fitful music on stolen Pan pipes
Arouses the meandering south wind,
Awakens the sleeping buds, and
Calls to puddle-happy people.

But it is only March and
The cruel imp giggles gleefully as
He instructs his winter brother to
Halt the wind,
Put the buds to sleep,
And freeze the happy-people's puddles.

(Published in *Baptist Student*)

===

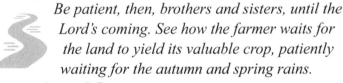 *Be patient, then, brothers and sisters, until the
Lord's coming. See how the farmer waits for
the land to yield its valuable crop, patiently
waiting for the autumn and spring rains.*
James 5:7

*...then I will send rain on your land in its season, both
autumn and spring rains, so that you may gather in your
grain, new wine and olive oil.*

Deuteronomy 11:14
Be glad, people of Zion, rejoice in the LORD your God,
for He has given you the autumn rains because He is
faithful. He sends you abundant showers, both autumn
and spring rains, as before.
Joel 2: 23

Meanderings: Have you ever been
impatient to move on to the next
season? How do you see the Lord
providing during the various seasons?

Father, In the winter of life, we await... we welcome
spring. And yet, help me to not be impatient with the
season that I am in. There is much valuable about being
in the winter, harsh as it can be. I praise You for the
faithful change of seasons and what each has to offer
me.

To God be the glory

14. Dear Mr. Aborigine

Mr. Aborigine, I'm scared.
The little boys are playing war games again
And the new boy stepped across Tom's line.

Can I come live with you?
You don't have a house like mine.
But I don't have a house like mine,
Anymore
Either.

===

 Peace I leave with you; My peace I give you. I do not give to you as the world gives. Do not let your hearts be troubled and do not be afraid.
John 14:27

You will hear of wars and rumors of wars, but see to it that you are not alarmed. Such things must happen, but the end is still to come.
Matthew 24:6

They will beat their swords into plowshares and their spears into pruning hooks. Nation will not take up sword against nation, nor will they train for war anymore.
Isaiah 2: 4

Meanderings: What is your reaction
when you hear of wars and situations
that seem as if the world is ending?
Or out of control? How do you rely on
God during these times?

*Father, we live in a world of such chaos! Such violence!
Such anxiety! Such evil! We need Your peace, Your
perfect peace.   I don't want the wimpy peace that is
mindlessly tossed out by the world. Please... Your
peace... everlasting... eternal. Help me rely on You
when I hear of wars. Help me remember that this is all
in Your perfect time.*

To God be the glory

15. Mirror

Do I look old?
Do you see sorrow
Framed in my face?
Am I gray;
Do I wrinkle?
Do I weep the rheum
Of the aged?

My mirror
Is partial;
I dare not trust it
For I would die
Of slow veins
And molding bones.

Is this the plan?
The shattering rendition
Of a life in decrescendo…
Of a soul into breath-thin marble?
===

I am weathered but still elegant,
oh, dear sisters in Jerusalem,
Weather-darkened like Kedar desert tents,
time-softened like Solomon's Temple hangings.
Don't look down on me because I'm dark,
darkened by the sun's harsh rays.

My brothers ridiculed me and sent me to work in the fields. They made me care for the face of the earth, but I had no time to care for my own face.
Song of Songs 1: 5-6

So even to old age and gray hairs, O God, do not forsake me, until I proclaim Your might to another generation, Your power to all those to come.
Psalm 71:18

Meanderings: How do you feel about aging? Do you embrace it or fight it? What lessons can you learn from growing older?

Father, Growing old is not an accident, a mistake, a mutation. It's not an option. Rather, it is a stage of life where I remember Who You were in years past, Who You are now, and Who You promise to be in years to come. Help me embrace the process, find the beauty of aging. Thank You for the years. Help me pass on to my grandchildren the joy of the years.

To God be the glory

16. Pizzicato Nocturne

Ragged chords and lone notes
Come to harmony
As the first movement journeys to the last.

The wandering aria,
The lost adagio
Sweep to symphony
With the master and the harp
One in finale.

Only the rhapsody
Remains,
Wavering into thin echoes.

==

 *Whenever the spirit from God came on Saul,
David would take up his lyre and play. Then
relief would come to Saul; he would feel
better, and the evil spirit would leave him.*
1 Samuel 16: 23

*Addressing one another in psalms and hymns and
spiritual songs, singing and making melody to the Lord
with your heart.*
Ephesians 5:19

How lovely is Your dwelling place,
O LORD of hosts!
My soul longs, yes, faints
for the courts of the LORD;
my heart and flesh sing for joy
to the living God.
Psalm 84: 1-2

Meanderings: How is music powerful in your life? Does it move you to pray? To sing? To ponder? Like David's harp, does it give soothing relief? Do you sing for joy to God?

Father, the power of music! The power to heal, to comfort, to encourage! Such power that even as the last note disappears, applause arises and the memory is carried. Thank You for music to praise You!

To God be the glory

17. Shadows

Vague shadows fall tonight
Smudging the little boundaries
Between languages.

Shadows fall,
Hiding faces,
Marring valleys and mountains.

They all are alike
When the moon prowls the cloudy sky.

===

*I appeal to you, brothers and sisters, in the
name of our Lord Jesus Christ, that all of you
agree with one another in what you say and
that there be no divisions among you, but that
you be perfectly united in mind and thought.*
1 Corinthians 1:10

*But avoid foolish controversies, genealogies,
dissensions, and quarrels about the law, for they are
unprofitable and worthless. As for a person who stirs up
division, after warning him once and then twice, have
nothing more to do with him, knowing that such a person
is warped and sinful; he is self-condemned.*
Titus 3: 9-11

Meanderings: What are some of the divisions and boundaries in your life? How do you cross boundaries for the sake of the gospel?

Father, help us to seek You. We want You to be the center of our unity. We seek Your holiness, Your perfect name. Help us stand strong for You. Forgive me when I do not always see all mankind in need of You, when I ignore some. Remind me, Father, that we are precious to You.

To God be the glory

18. On My Way to the Barn

I. Where they threw the garbage
In the fall,
Grow squash and corn
And tomatoes
In the spring.

II. When they ground corn,
Soft white dust
Covered cobwebs, old harness, gunny sacks
Looking like snow
On a picture postcard.

III. Why a leaning fence
Even after all the hasty repairs?
Rabbits and squirrels and cats
Scuttle under the bottom board,
While the calf noses a possible escape.

IV. How the dusky shadows
Meld with the barn!
Faded red boards
In juxtaposition with
Sunset strata.
And then the first star
Pierces through the pattern.

====================================

*There is a time for everything,
and a season for every activity under the
heavens.*
Ecclesiastes 3:1

*But ask the animals, and they will teach you, or the birds
in the sky, and they will tell you; or speak to the earth,
and it will teach you, or let the fish in the sea inform you.
Which of all these does not know that the hand of the
LORD has done this?   In His hand is the life of every
creature and the breath of all mankind.*
Job 12: 7-10

Meanderings: What scenes do you see
outside that remind you of the power
and glory of God? Has an animal
ever taught you an important lesson?

*Father, I am thankful for being raised in the country, so
close to Your creation. Thank You for creating in me a
curious and adventuring spirit, seeking the questions, the
answers, and beauty of the farm. Thank You for
teaching me the wonder of birth and death on the farm.
Help me see You in all! I praise Your holy name for the
many pictures and scenes outside.*

To God be the glory

19. The Potter's Work

Ceramic faces in shards…
Fragmented in the dust heaps,
Toppled like vases
Wobbling from mantle to hearth.

Yet once,
They were
Soft warm clay
Yielded, ready for tender sculpting,
A firm touch,
A breath of life.

==

*But now, O LORD, You are our Father; We are
the clay, and You our potter; And all we are
the work of Your hand.*
Isaiah 64:8

*And the vessel he was making of clay was spoiled in the
potter's hand, and he reworked it into another vessel, as
it seemed good to the potter to do.*
Jeremiah 18:4

Meanderings: How difficult to watch
someone descend into something less
than intended! How do you, as a clay

vessel, stay strong and useful for the Lord? How do you reach out to those who are shattered?

Father, Creator! Author! Alpha and Omega! Beginning and End! From dust to dust, teach me to count my days, and give praise. Remind me that You are in control; You create and mold me. I pray that my life will always be a testament of You.

To God be the glory

20. City Walls at Night

Bright orange high-rise windows
So square in the cobalt sky
Like a museum checkerboard.

And if we squint
We see tiny window washers
Polishing away city grime.

And if we blink
We see them as
Dancers pulsing in
Orange and blue
Strobe lights.

And if we stare wide eyed
Tears stream
Riveting orange and blue rivers
Blending down the checkerboard.

==

*Do you not know? Have you not heard? ...It is
He who sits above the circle of the earth, And
its inhabitants are like grasshoppers, Who
stretches out the heavens like a curtain, And
spreads them out like a tent to dwell in.*
Isaiah 40:21-22

The eyes of the Lord are in every place, keeping watch on the evil and the good.
Proverbs 15:3

The Lord looks down from heaven; He sees all the children of man
Psalm 33:13

Meanderings: What does a child think when he/she looks up at you? What does God see when He looks at you?

Father, I will never see the world as You see it. You, seated on high, above all, see all. You know all. You know my name and my life. This is indeed my Father's world. Help me to wait on You. Help make my life to be inspiring to those who look at me... for them to see You living in me.

To God be the glory

21. June Morning

Sticky June mornings sit on my chest
Crushing my lungs into liquid air.
I jolt awake, the angry Van Gogh sun
Glaring through my window.
I suck breath.
Butter legs and arms melt into sweat-damp sheets.

Heavy thump-ticks of the clock rattle my ears
And I skim the beaded sweat on my lip.

===

Let me hear in the morning of Your steadfast
*   love,*
*   for in You I trust.*
*   Make me know the way I should go,*
for to You I lift up my soul.
Psalm 143:8

The steadfast love of the Lord never ceases; His mercies
never come to an end; they are new every morning; great
is Your faithfulness.
Lamentations 3:22-23

But I, O Lord, cry to You; in the morning my prayer
comes before You.
Psalm 88:13

Meanderings: Are you a morning person? What are your first thoughts and actions when you awaken? What can be your morning prayer?

Father, remind me to seek You, to inquire of You first, and not let the days and circumstances pull me down. Even on the hard days, especially the hard days, nudge me to pray for Your grace and guidance. Before I even leave my bed, help me to remember that You are in perfect control.

To God be the glory

22. Green Cherries

Green cherries caught in blush,
Balls of wax among blue leaves
Await soft sun's lips.

==

 *Abide in Me, and I in You. As the branch
cannot bear fruit of itself unless it abides in
the vine, so neither can you unless you abide
in Me.*
John 15:4-5

*Though the fig tree does not bud
and there are no grapes on the vines,
though the olive crop fails
and the fields produce no food,
though there are no sheep in the pen
and no cattle in the stalls,
yet I will rejoice in the Lord,
I will be joyful in God my Savior.*
Habakkuk 3: 17-18

Meanderings: Do you keep plants?
Have you had the experience of the
plant dying? How do you keep your
plants strong and thriving? What

parallels do you see in this and in your spiritual life?

Father, Creator of all nature, I thank You for the lessons of the fruit. Thank You for teaching me that I must be rooted in You. Thank You for reminding me of Your perfect timing. Help me to continue to be joyful even when it seems as if Your timing is not perfect; help me be patient and wait on You.

To God be the glory

23. The Stylus

The crow with silent wings
Flies over my face
Night after night,
Dragging one foot
First this way,
Then that…
To engrave etchings about my eyes.

===

 Even when I am old and gray,
  do not forsake me, my God,
  'til I declare Your power to the next
  generation,
Your mighty acts to all who are to come.
Psalm 71:1

*Therefore we do not lose heart. Though outwardly we
are wasting away, yet inwardly we are being renewed
day by day.*
2 Corinthians 4:8

*I will be your God throughout your lifetime -- until your
hair is white with age. I made you, and I will care for
you. I will carry you along and save you*
Isaiah 46:4

Meanderings: Do you fear growing old? As you age, what do you see God doing in your life? Has your purpose changed over the years?

Father, You have not forgotten me; You still provide and protect. Thank You for the gift of years, for the privilege of growing old. I cling to Your promises of always being there.

To God be the glory

24. Popcorn

1966.
My boyfriend is measuring corn and oil.
We shake the rattling pan over the burner,
In rhythm to *Little Deuce Coupe.*
Mouth watering, eyes meeting,
We settle down to hot buttered bliss.
My mother hovers.

1975.
He appears uninvited at my wedding,
Questions in his eyes,
Congratulations and popcorn stories in his mouth.
My mother hovers.

==

 *For I know the plans that I have for you,
declares the Lord, plans for welfare and not
for calamity, to give you a future and a hope.
Jeremiah 29:11*

*Every good and perfect gift is from above, coming down
from the Father of the heavenly lights, Who does not
change like shifting shadows.
James 1:17*

Meanderings: What plans are you discovering that the Lord has been unfolding in your life? Have there been times that relationships had to change so that you could be in God's perfect plans?

Father, what a difference time makes! Thank You for allowing us to change and grow within the safety of Your perfect will and time. And yet, we praise You for being the One that never changes. Thank You for Your perfect plans. Sometimes I think I know the plan... and then find that You have something different for me, something better for me.

To God be the glory

25. Volkswagen Students... Buick Teacher (the used car lot in Room 101)

I. What am I, invisible?
My light are on; my horn is blaring.
I share the road, just
Don't rub your big Buick on my paint.
Don't wrap your tires around my rims.
Leave my rust in your dust.
I'll choke on your smoke when
You sideswipe my fenders and peel out
So's I'll never catch up.
No dings, no benders,
This buggy's fine, just fine, so
You stay on your side
Of the white dotted line,
And I'll stay on mine.

II. I suppose you already know my plate number
And have memorized every pit in my shiny paint job.
But you don't know my road music:
How my engine hums
When it's clean and mean,
How the brake drums pound out bass
And the wiper rhythms on a rainy day
Metronome the drops away,
Or hear my radio play.
Have you ever heard my radio play?

III. Someday I wanna be a Lincoln,
Big stretch limo, chrome bright wheels
With a uniform in front
And leather seat and black glass.
Man, oh man, ain't it gonna be grand,
Passing that Buick.

IV. A flat.
Can't believe I got a flat.
No jack, no spare.
Just as I'm about to catch the Buick,
I'm limping off, ripping tread,
Leaking air.
I just wanted to be on the road, you know,
Just movin',
But now I got a flat,
And no Triple A bandaid's
Gonna fix that.

===

*Just as a body, though one, has many parts,
but all its many parts form one body, so it is
with Christ. For we were all baptized by one
Spirit so as to form one body—whether Jews
or Gentiles, slave or free—and we were all given the one
Spirit to drink. Even so the body is not made up of one
part but of many.*
1 Corinthians 12:12-14

My brothers and sisters, believers in our glorious Lord Jesus Christ must not show favoritism. Suppose a man comes into your meeting wearing a gold ring and fine clothes, and a poor man in filthy old clothes also comes in. If you show special attention to the man wearing fine clothes and say, 'Here's a good seat for you,' but say to the poor man, 'You stand there' or 'Sit on the floor by my feet,' have you not discriminated among yourselves and become judges with evil thoughts?
James 2:1-4

Meanderings: Do you tend to judge others? Is it difficult to see those in a group as being individuals? How can you see each as God's creation?

Father, it was a joy, a privilege, and a sober responsibility to be a teacher. Thank You for teaching me to see each student as an individual, and that each, no matter what, was precious in your sight. Help me to continue to see the people around me as Your creation, as people who need You.

To God be the glory

26. Listen for the Whistle

"River's risin'," observed the old man
At the gas station.
"They say it's gonna beat '72."
"They say Alexandria went under.
"They say more rain's a comin'.

The spring rains that washed away the snows
Turn into summer rains, relentless pounding rains,
Saturating the land,
Drowning farmer's dreams.
Floods crawled under fences, crept throughout barns,
Defied dams.
So we sandbagged at Pin Oaks Levee,
Trying to trick the Mississippi.

National Guard officers,
(boys really, official and scared)
Stopped us on the road.
"Who are you?"
"Why are you here?"
"Where are you headed?"
They waved us on.

Another told us how to park.
"Facing out,
Keys in ignition,
Ready to roll when the whistle blows."

Another gave us gloves, shovels, plastic bags,
And pointed to the sand pile.
"Fill to here.
Shake it down.
Fold it under."

We joined the rhythmic scooping of sand.
Crunch, slap, fold, toss.
Crunch, slap, fold, toss.
Teen boys on daddy's tractors
Pulled flat trailers to load for the levees
And the patching boats.
We listened for the whistle.

Snakes slithered through the weeds.
"Been a lot of snakes this year,
runnin' from the river."
We listened for the whistle.

Sand fleas scurried up our pants,
Biting around sock cuffs and waist bands.
Slap, scratch, wipe sweat.
Brush sand out of eyes.
Slap, scratch, wipe sweat.
Brush sand out of eyes.
We listened for the whistle.

Red Cross ladies waded out.

Sandwiches, tinny-tasting cans of juice,
Coffee, coffee, coffee.
In the barn, children leaped on filled bags,
Sleeping babies fidgeted in baskets
Near their shoveling mothers.
We listened for the whistle.

Reports filtered in:
"Dam broke at Foley."
"Elsberry's going under."
"Rose three inches last hour."

The teen boys rumored gushy ground,
Leaks in the levee.
Thunderheads piled in the western sky,
Green and yellow skies,
Flickers of lightning,
Ominous thunder.

Crunch, slap, fold, toss.
Crunch, slap, fold, toss.
We heard the slapping of the waters,
Waves beating the levee,
Slapping of the sand hitting the bag,
Slapping of the hand on sand fleas.

Night fell slowly, steamy Missouri nights
When the air is too thick to breathe,
When the shirt on the back never dries,
When a salty stream drips into already watering eyes.

From somewhere, a whip-poor-will began a cadence
And an owl screamed.
We jumped, threw down shovels,
Before realizing it was not the whistle.

We bagged by the lingering, melting sun,
By the growing flashes in the sky,
Then by tractor lights.
Coffee, coffee, coffee.
Slap, slap, slap.

Blisters built, broke, built, broke and bled.
Boat lights bobble across the waters.
We listened for the whistle.

"Go home." It was the National Guard officer.
"Go home. I'll take over here."

And even when we slept in our dry beds
On high ground,
We listened for the whistle.

And when the levee broke,
Weaseling through the tiniest of cracks,
Spewing ugly waters through the sandpile,
Suffocating 14,000 acres,
We listened for the whistle.

We listen for the whistle.
===

The Lord sits enthroned over the flood; the Lord sits enthroned as king forever. May the Lord give strength to His people! May the Lord bless His people with peace!
Psalm 29:10-11

In the six hundredth year of Noah's life, in the second month, on the seventeenth day of the month, on that day all the fountains of the great deep burst forth, and the windows of the heavens were opened.
Genesis 7:11

I establish my covenant with you, that never again shall all flesh be cut off by the waters of the flood, and never again shall there be a flood to destroy the earth."
Genesis 9:11

Meanderings: Have you ever faced a natural disaster? Did you call out to the Lord? Could you remember that He was in charge? How did you reach out to help others?

Father, I praise You for Your promise of never again destroying the earth by flood waters. It was hard to remember the promise as we worked on sandbags at the levee. It was hard to remember the promise when we saw people lose their homes and livelihood. It was hard to remember the promise when we saw fear of the creeping waters coming closer. But Your promises are real. Thank You for Your protection in the flood.

To God be the glory

27. O Grandpa...

When you lay shivering white,
I stroked your papery hand
And smelled death, lingering in sterile sheets,
Lurking in tubes and blinking monitors.

I wanted to take your hand,
Go pick cherries again,
Carry the bucket,
Watch your fingers, nimble among the ripe reds.

I wanted to take your hand,
Make birdhouses again,
Hand you nails,
Watch your grip, strong as oak.

But I smelled death, loitering in the hall,
Couched in shushed whispers.
So I held your withered hand,
Tracing the calluses,
Feeling your great gnarled knuckles.

I smelled death, closer now,
The sweet warm fragrance beckoning, inviting,
As I felt your stiffened fingers stretch, reach, lift...
So I let you go.

==

Jesus said to her, "I am the resurrection and the life. Whoever believes in Me, though he die, yet shall he live.
John 11:25

He will wipe away every tear from their eyes, and death shall be no more, neither shall there be mourning, nor crying, nor pain anymore, for the former things have passed away."
Revelation 21:4

Precious in the sight of the Lord is the death of His saints.
Psalm 116:15

Meanderings: It is difficult to face the death of a loved one. Is it easier for you to deal with the death of one who knows the Lord? How do you come to grips with the reality of death? How do you offer comfort to those facing death? To his or her family?

Father, I praise You for the Christian life and testament of my grandfather. It is hard to let go, yet… knowing that he enjoys Heaven with You, knowing that he has no more pain or sorrow, knowing that he is alive through faith in You for evermore… is comforting to my soul. Thank You for taking us through the dark valleys and into the light of Your truth and comfort.

To God be the glory

28. Like the Wind

Like the wind,
Swirling dust and snow into blinding whorls,
Raising and crashing the waves
That grind ocean stones into fine sand,
Filling sails and powering mills,

Uprooting mighty forests,
Smoothing jagged mountains
Into rounded mounds,
Lifting kites, carrying birds,

Whispering in the alleys,
Seeking the empty spots,
Filling the lowest crevice.

Like the wind,
Such is the holiness of God.

===

*For behold, He who forms mountains and
creates the wind
And declares to man what are His thoughts,
He who makes dawn into darkness
And treads on the high places of the earth,
The Lord God of hosts is His name.
Amos 4:13*

*He causes the vapors to ascend from the ends of the
earth;*
Who makes lightnings for the rain,
Who brings forth the wind from His treasuries.
Psalm 135:7

Worship the Lord in holy attire;
Tremble before Him, all the earth.
Psalm 96:9

"There is no one holy like the Lord,
Indeed, there is no one besides You,
Nor is there any rock like our God.
1 Samuel 2:2

Meanderings: Holiness! How difficult
to comprehend the full extent of God's
holiness! How does the wind show
attributes of God? How does God's
power and holiness affect your life?

Father, You are holy! Your power and might are more than I can comprehend, more than I understand. Yet I believe. Your holiness is my hope. You write that I am to be holy as You are holy. I know I can never attain Your holiness, yet You tell me to imitate You. I need You, Lord, and your power to be in this world. I need you even as the earth needs the wind to shape and create who You want me to be.

To God be the glory

29. Little Lost Man

He waits myopically by the stairs,
Seeing neither up nor down,
Little lost man
With Papillion eyes
And Rainman shuffle.
He cries Willie Loman tears.

Still he stands
Ignoring the hands
That try to pat away the fear.

Mrs. Robinson, where are you?
Mrs. Kramer, call home.

===

 For God gave us a spirit not of fear but of
power and love and self-control.
2 Timothy 1:7

But they who wait for the Lord shall renew their
strength; they shall mount up with wings like eagles;
they shall run and not be weary; they shall walk and not
faint.
Isaiah 40:31

He gives power to the faint, and to him who has no might
He increases strength.
Isaiah 40:29

Therefore do not worry about tomorrow, for tomorrow
will worry about itself. Each day has enough trouble of
its own.
Matthew 6:34

A joyful heart is good medicine, but a crushed spirit
dries up the bones.
Proverbs 17:22

Meanderings: Do you know some of the lost, forgotten, and confused people in this world? How do you show Jesus to them? How do you help them overcome fear?

Father, so many of the arts and pieces of literature give
me pause to reflect on You. Lost characters with
overwhelming fear, with no hope, and no understanding
of You make me grateful for You in my life. My life could
have been filled with fear, weakness, weariness, worry,
and a crushed spirit. You alone, O God, have the power
to make me whole and fulfilled.

To God be the glory

30. Prayers From Building This House

I.   Prayers of Glass

I live in a glass world
Of mirrors and shards,
Windows and lights,
And tricks of the night.

I look through my neighbor.
He looks through me.
We do not see each other.

I look through sacred words;
They elude me.

Lord,
Help me see clearly
Past the flaws and
Wavy distortions.
Let me see the reflection of You.

II. Prayers of Brick

The bricks defeat me,
Weigh me down,
Lowly bits of clay and straw
Yet heavy in my hod.

God,
Let me build the walls
Strong and mortared,
Lasting for generations
With the bricks You hand me.

III. Prayers of Wood

Splinters,
Rough sawn sheets of lumber
Await the plane.

Lord,
Sand me smooth,
Anoint me with Your oil,
Rubbed to the finish.

Let me yield
To the Carpenter.

===

O afflicted one, storm-tossed, and not
comforted,
Behold, I will set your stones in antimony,
And your foundations I will lay in sapphires.
Isaiah 54:11

For we know that if the earthly tent which is our house is torn down, we have a building from God, a house not made with hands, eternal in the heavens.
2 Corinthians 5:1

For we are God's fellow workers; you are God's field, God's building.
1 Corinthians 3:9

Therefore encourage one another and build up one another, just as you also are doing.
1 Thessalonians 5:11

Unless the Lord builds the house, those who build it labor in vain. Unless the Lord watches over the city, the watchman stays awake in vain.
Psalm 127:1

Whatever you do, work heartily, as for the Lord and not for men
Colossians 3:23

Meanderings: Have you ever started a project without understanding exactly how to do it? Did you ask the Lord to equip and guide you on this venture? How has the Lord been fashioning and building you?

Father, when I try to build something on my own, I often fail. Perhaps I did not even begin by asking You for guidance. Perhaps I began to think I could do it myself. Perhaps I began to follow my own guidelines, and not Yours. Help me to remember that You are in charge. Help me do Your work with all my might and strength. Help me go back to the blue prints of Your Word.

To God be the glory

31. The Cherry Tree

The ice storm toppled the cherry tree
The morning Grandma died.
The heavy trunk still hung by a splinter to the root
While the twiggy top brushed into the snow.

After the funeral we returned to the farm
To feast on ham sandwiches from the church ladies.
Charles ate pie at the kitchen window.

"That tree," he pointed the wedge of pie at the toppled
tree, *"That tree will have to wait until spring. Too cold
now."*
Grandpa only nodded.

But as spring fields cautiously turned green,
So green-slow that one had to stop and look again,
And check for brown,
The cherry tree greened,
blossomed,
Reddened into summer.

And so it cycled,
Year after year,
Until Grandpa died
And we cut up the cherry tree.

(Dedicated to Wilda and Ernest Newquist, my grandparents)

======================================

Place me like a seal over your heart,
like a seal on your arm;
for love is as strong as death,
its jealousy unyielding as the grave.
It burns like blazing fire,
like a mighty flame.
Song of Songs 8:6

Yet there will be a tenth portion in it,
And it will again be subject to burning,
Like a terebinth or an oak
Whose stump remains when it is felled.
The holy seed is its stump.
Isaiah 6:13

Meanderings: Is there an object that represents the love you have for another? The love you have for God? That God has for you? What memories does this object bring? How can you share this with others?

Father, Thank You for this miracle of the cherry tree, and how it reminds me of Your love for us. Thank You for the example of love between my grandparents, and again of how it represented Your love. Thank You for being that lasting root of our spiritual lives. Help me to pass on this miracle and love to those around me.

To God be the glory

32. Wise Old Stones

I must cross this river to your little house,
The contrary, confounding river
Of confusing twists and contorted bends.

No bridge exists.

Years ago
One may have crossed where the banks lean in,
Narrowing the gap.
But the past is the past
And no bridge exists.

Stones cross the river here,
Broad flat stones worn smooth by rough waters,
Old wise stone now in deep still waters.

Upstream raw water still rushes
Along the shallows,
Beating on young sharp rocks
That jut their jaws against the foam.

I ponder the excitement there:
Pounding of the vein,
Shooting rapids,
Cataract surge,
Burst of spray glinting into silver.

Then I turn to the old stones,
These silent clear waiting stones
Where the water is deep but still.

I must cross this river to your little house,
And the old stones will take me there.

==

And Joshua said to the people of Israel, "When your children ask their fathers in times to come, 'What do these stones mean?' then you shall let your children know, 'Israel passed over this Jordan on dry ground.' For the Lord your God dried up the waters of the Jordan for you until you passed over, as the Lord your God did to the Red Sea, which He dried up for us until we passed over, so that all the peoples of the earth may know that the hand of the Lord is mighty, that you may fear the Lord your God forever."
Joshua 4: 21-24

Do not move an ancient boundary stone set up by your ancestors.   Proverbs 22:28

Meanderings: Do you have "stones" in your life that give you a foundation? How can you let the next generation know of these stones?

Father, the permanence and strength and resilience of stones have blessed me. Thank You for the stones you have placed along my path to remind me of what You have done in my life. Please let me use them to remind another generation of Your love and provision.

To God be the glory

33. 7 PM, September 1935

She tucked three little girls
Into one bed,
Pulled up quilts,
Kissed each forehead,
Tiptoed out.

In the kitchen
She swept the linoleum,
Threw another stick into the stove,
Pumped water from the cistern,
Boiled coffee,
Set the table for one
On a white starched doily,
Changed her apron.

In the parlor
She rocked,
Mending leggings by touch,
Gazed into lengthening shadows,
Humming.

He entered the kitchen,
Home from the mines,
Face and hands and overalls
As sooty as the dusk outside.

He placed his battered black lunch pail
On the table by the doily,
Rolled up his sleeves,
Splashed face and hands in the bucket
At the cistern sink,
Sat… coughing.
She laid out
Applesauce,
Thick slices of bread,
Cold milk with flecks of cream,
And shut the ice box door.

They prayed. And poured coffee.

He ate in silence,
She murmured about the girls,
The garden.
They kissed,
And he climbed the stairs,
Coughing,
Muttering about poor soil,
Poor air,
Coughing,
Coughing.
She washed and wiped the dishes,
Stretched out the towel to dry,
Hung up her apron.

It was time.

She sank into the old chair on the stones
Outside the kitchen door,
The two becoming one shape.

The sun was setting, almost finished,
Stretching purples, like ripe plums, across the horizon,
Blackening the barn against it.
She stretched out her fingers to the gathering darkness
And ignored the biting chill.

The whip-poor-will and frogs chorused,
Then stopped.
From inside the barn,
A calf bleated and the cows lowed a reply.
Chickens rustled down.
Somewhere, faintly, a dog yipped.

The purples faded, leaving muted grape stains.
She felt gentle dusk falling around her,
Caressing her shoulders, fingering her loose hair.
Darkness dissolved the barn into the sky.

She sighed.
It had been her time, her precious time.
Inside, she measured coffee grounds for morning,
And blew out the light.

(Dedicated to Freda and Clarence Glenn, my grandparents)

==

*When you pass through the waters, I will be
with you; and through the rivers, they shall
not overwhelm you; when you walk through
the fire you shall not be burned, and the flame
shall not consume you.
Isaiah 43:2*

*Strength and dignity are her clothing, and she laughs at
the time to come.
Proverbs 31:25*

*For I consider that the sufferings of this present time are
not worth comparing with the glory that is to be revealed
to us.
Romans 8:18*

Meanderings: Is there someone in
your family who sacrificed much to
give you life and what you needed in
life? How can you honor them?

*Father, Thank You for the example of these
grandparents, who bravely faced hard times, and
remained faithful to You. They worked, they prayed, they
loved, they did the best they could. And they relied on
You to carry them when the path became too rough. I
praise You for placing them in my life.*

To God be the glory

34. Pearls

I wonder:
Did you smile
As you marched jungle hills,
Bayonet glints matching the pace pace pace
Of stiff nervous boots?

Did you grimace an unbelieving grin
When hissing whispering bullets prowled your belly?
When you danced high in dust
And kissed steam-sponge earth?

Did the ringing jungle sun broil and split your lips?
Did biting flies swarm your teeth
Looking like braces and brackets when you were twelve?

Your smile is my pain without wax,
Shifting with pressure,
Rooted white and straight,
Bought at great price
Like rows of marble stones at Arlington.

==

*There is a time for everything,
and a season for every activity under the
heavens:
a time to be born and a time to die,
a time to plant and a time to uproot,*

a time to kill and a time to heal,
a time to tear down and a time to build,
a time to weep and a time to laugh,
a time to mourn and a time to dance,
a time to scatter stones and a time to gather them,
a time to embrace and a time to refrain from embracing,
a time to search and a time to give up,
a time to keep and a time to throw away,
a time to tear and a time to mend,
a time to be silent and a time to speak
a time to love and a time to hate,
a time for war and a time for peace.
Ecclesiastes 3: 3-8

Again, the kingdom of heaven is like a merchant seeking beautiful pearls, who, when he had found one pearl of great price, went and sold all that he had and bought it.
Matthew 13: 45-46

Meanderings: Have you known someone who died in war? Did that person have a noble sense of purpose? Was their death in vain? Consider Jesus. Was His death in vain?

Father, it is most difficult for me to fathom war, and the many lives lost in war.   It is hard for me to find purpose in the midst of horror.   Yet, You say that there are times for everything, including war.   The lives were costly; freedom isn't free. The pearl of Jesus Christ was costly; it cost His life.   Help me sell out to Jesus, this pearl of great price. Help me remember the sacrifices and the cost.

To God be the glory

35. Rabble
(A response to Luke 5: 1-11)

Shrill pitched shards of conversation
Cutting through the grumbling mumbles of the street,
Hawkers pitching their wares:
"Dates! Chickens! Olives, ripe olives!"

Screams of heedless children darting between tents,
Swearing sailors, sweaty, grimy, noisily tossing boxes,
Slapping ropes,
jostling, punching, greeting, nodding, leaving...
And the steady lapping of the waves against the boat.

Against this, the calm of one man,
Spreads like rings around a rock tossed into the sea.

I, Peter, Simon, Cephus, have no time for this soapbox.
There is work to be done!
No fish in the nets tonight,
No coins jingling
In my pocket,
Wash, mend, clean, repair... tomorrow will be better.

And now this man, the calm one, approaches me.
"Let's go out," he suggests.
Are you crazy? Can't you see? No fish!
Let's go out," he repeats.
Have it your way. I shrug, make ready.

"Lower your nets."
Truly, this man does not know fishing!
But compelling. So compelling.
We lower the nets.

The heaviness brings tears to my eyes.
Pull, tug, strain at the catch. Heave! Heave!
"Master!" I cry, *"Master!"*

I stop, aghast.
This man, the calm one, the crazy one…
And I called him "Master"?

He simply looks at me as if he expected it.
"Peter."
He knows my name!
"Peter."
His voice is strong, bold.
"Peter. The catch is good. But it is not all you will catch. Someday… you will catch men."

Indeed, he is crazy. I don't understand.
But I believe him. For some crazy reason, I believe.

"Follow, follow me."
(I don't know how.)

"Follow, follow me."
(I'm scared.)

"Follow, follow me."
(Here I am, Lord. Use me.)

(Published in *The Way*, February 1989)

===

 *Now faith is confidence in what we hope for
and assurance about what we do not see.
Hebrews 11:1*

*I have chosen the way of faithfulness;
I have set my heart on Your laws.
Psalm 119:30*

*You did not choose Me, but I chose you and appointed
you so that you might go and bear fruit—fruit that will
last—and so that whatever you ask in My name the
Father will give you.
John 15:16*

Meanderings: Has God ever asked you
to do the impossible?   How did you
decide to either obey or go your own
way?   How is Peter an example to
you?

Father, in so many ways, I am like Peter. Faithful.... Unfaithful. Cautious in where I place my faith. Not always understanding. The Word gives me such joy in seeing Peter transformed! He began to understand that he was chosen for something far greater than himself, and he became a man of great faith... a fisher of men. Lord, I may never be of the caliber of Peter, but his story gives me hope that I can remain steadfast in my calling. Help me say from day to day that I have chosen the way of faithfulness. Help me be reassured of Your presence in my life each day.

To God be the glory

36. The Promised Land

Sadie arranges bagels behind bakery windows
And watches five o'clock December descend
On 59th Street.
Across the street,
The red, cracked leatherette cafe
Lies sandwiched between Paradise Hotel
And Goldie's Haberdashery.

Soon the old ones gather
Under the sagging chandelier in the Paradise:
Orange faced women with purple -streaked legs,
Teary-eyed men clutching canes.
Rudy asks Betty to take his arm;
Maxie stumbles over his own cuffs;
Sybil drops her gloves; Marge drools.

The five o'clock wind blows leaves between their legs,
Tangles papers in the gutter,
And makes Rudy pray for a coat.
Betty will open the door; Maxie will close it.
Marge will spill coffee; Sybil will fumble for a napkin.

Sadie watches them
Ritual to the cafe.
She locks the register,
And turns *Open* into *Sorry, Closed.*

===

See, how good and how pleasing it is for
brothers to live together as one! It is like oil
of great worth poured on the head, flowing
down through the hair on the face, even the face
of Aaron, and flowing down to his coat.
Psalm 133:1-3

And let us consider how we may spur one another on
toward love and good deeds, not giving up meeting
together, as some are in the habit of doing, but
encouraging one another—and all the more as you see
the Day approaching.
Hebrews 10:24–25

All the believers were together and had everything in
common. They sold property and possessions to give to
anyone who had need. Every day they continued to meet
together in the temple courts. They broke bread in their
homes and ate together with glad and sincere hearts,
praising God and enjoying the favor of all the people.
And the Lord added to their number daily those who
were being saved.
Acts 2: 44-47

For just as each of us has one body with many members,
and these members do not all have the same function, so
in Christ we, though many, form one body, and each
member belongs to all the others.
Romans 12: 4-5

Meanderings: Are you part of a community? A neighborhood? A church? How do you and the members help each other? Why did God create us to live in community? What are the advantages or disadvantages of being part of a community?

Father, As I ponder the concept of living as a community, I take great joy in reading of the early apostles, their vibrant faith, and their love for each other. Please give us the essence of community in our churches and in our lives. Help me reach out to others, especially those who are like-minded. There is strength in kindred spirits being together for Your glory!

To God be the glory

37. Shadow Dove

Holy wars fought in Your name
Were, after all, only wars
Of human pride, greed, power,
Leaving slivers
Of hate and misunderstandings
Scattered among the minarets, spires, and onion domes
Of the centuries… of the lands.

But to call on Your name:
Rose of Sharon, Lion of Judah,
Prince of Peace, Emmanuel,
Lamb,
Shepherd,
Lord, Father, Son, Savior, Redeemer,
El Shaddai, Abba, Friend
Infuses me with Your power,
Changes my life.

Your words become mine,
Trembling this clay vessel.

Descend on me, Holy Spirit,
Like a dove
With Your pentecostal power,
Like a flame dancing on my head.
Soar me to the hills on eagle's wings.

I have no need
Of holy wars
When I can find God waiting for me
On lonely porches,
Singing to me
In the wind,
Crying to me
As a hungry child.

The choosing of my mind,
The battle of my conscience,
The struggle of right and wrong,
The trumpet call of my own greed

Are war enough.

===

 Do nothing out of selfish ambition or vain conceit. Rather, in humility value others above yourselves
Philippians 2:3

Let us therefore make every effort to do what leads to peace and to mutual edification.
Romans 14:19

Bear with each other and forgive one another if any of you has a grievance against someone. Forgive as the Lord forgave you. And over all these virtues put on love, which binds them all together in perfect unity.
Colossians 3:13-14

Meanderings: Sometimes the war of my conscience permeates my life. Do you struggle with making the right choice? Doing the right thing? Serving others who never show that they care? How can you win this war and live in grace?

Father, sometimes it is hard for me to imagine all believers in perfect unity. Believers in Jesus, everywhere... every part of the globe.... Living in peace with one another, forgiving without hesitation, loving, no divisions, no arguments, living in humility, encouraging and building each other up. Lord, hasten the day. And meanwhile please give me grace, and help me see others as You do.

To God be the glory

38. Just So Romantic

"Oh, Harry. This just thrills me."
"Huh?"
"Why, this is so romantic. I just feel like a girl again."
"Well, now."
"O Harry. Just listen to that sax."
"Sax?"
"O Harry. I just close my eyes and think
Of that social when you told me I had nice legs."
"Lela, back then I couldn't even SEE your legs."
"Don't you remember? You walked me home that night,
And you said… you said I had a beautiful ankle.
And I said, 'Oh, go on, Harry Appleby. I bet say say that
to all the girls.'
And you know what, Harry?"
"What, Lela?"
"You did. You really did. You went on."
"Lela?"
"Yes, Harry?"
"Would you like this dance?"
"Oh, Harry. This is just so romantic."

===

However, let each one of you love his wife as himself, and let the wife see that she respects her husband.
Ephesians 5:33

An excellent wife who can find? She is far more precious than jewels.
Proverbs 31:10

I am my beloved's and my beloved is mine.
Song of Songs 6:3

Two are better than one, because they have a good reward for their toil.
Ecclesiastes 4:9

Love is patient, love is kind. It does not envy, it does not boast, it is not proud. It does not dishonor others, it is not self-seeking, it is not easily angered, it keeps no record of wrongs.
1 Corinthians 13: 4-5

Meanderings: How did you meet your spouse? How do you show respect? What attributes of your spouse are most precious to you? How are the two of you better than one?

Father, I am so blessed with the wonderful husband You gave me. My marriage is a blessing! Thank You for helping us learn to love each other, and to do so with You as the head of this union. Help us learn to forgive, to honor, to continue hand in hand. Help us to grow in rejoicing together.

To God be the glory

39. Laughter…

… Like sweet crushed
Summer peaches
Lingers in her voice.

==

 *A joyful heart is good medicine, but a crushed
spirit dries up the bones.*
Proverbs 17:22

*Then our mouth was filled with laughter, and our
tongue with shouts of joy; then they said among the
nations, "The Lord has done great things for them."*
Psalm 126:2

*He will yet fill your mouth with laughter, and your lips
with shouting.*
Job 8:21

Blessed are you who weep now, for you shall laugh.
Luke 6:21

Meanderings: Is laughter a part of
your day? Do you share laughter with
others? What brings laughter to you?

Father, Laughter!! Not crude jokes, or misplaced and inappropriate humor. Not laughing at, but laughing with. Pure laughter spilling from our smiles. Laughter that uplifts. Laughter that is contagious. Laughter that leads to happy tears. Thank You for the gift of laughter. I cannot imagine a world without the language of laughing.

To God be the glory

40. Purple Shadows

These easy purple shadows
Fall languidly beneath
Blue afternoons.

I trudge to the garden
Behind the spring pool
In a broken dance of time,
Pulling purple shadows behind me.

==

 God saw that the light was good, and He separated the light from the darkness. God called the light "day," and the darkness He called "night."
Genesis 1:4

A generation goes, and a generation comes, but the earth remains forever. The sun rises, and the sun goes down, and hastens to the place where it rises.
Ecclesiastes 1: 4-5

The whole earth is filled with awe at Your wonders; where morning dawns, where evening fades, You call forth songs of joy.
Psalm 65:8

Meanderings: In a broken world, God provides rhythms of constancy and faithfulness. What natural rhythms give structure and comfort to you?

Father, Your creation and timing are perfect... exquisite. I never have to worry about whether the sun will rise or if it will set. I can relax, knowing that You have the world in Your control. I can enjoy the beauty of the skies at sunset, and praise Your name! Even when time seems broken, I can look to Your patterns in creation, and rejoice.

To God be the glory

41. Near the Lake...

...winter winds play
With summer's death
I am a prisoner
Staring through eternity's window.

===

 And this is eternal life, that they know You, the only true God, and Jesus Christ whom You have sent.
John 17:3

Whoever believes in the Son has eternal life; whoever does not obey the Son shall not see life, but the wrath of God remains on him.
John 3:36

And after you have suffered a little while, the God of all grace, Who has called you to His eternal glory in Christ, will Himself restore, confirm, strengthen, and establish you.
1 Peter 5:10

Meanderings: What season of life are you in? Does the process of growing older sometimes overwhelm you? Does the concept of eternity seem impossible, or even frightening?   How can God calm your heart through His Word?

Father, yes, I grow older, from summer to winter. Yes, I sometimes feel as if I am stuck, waiting for eternity. And yet... Your plans are perfect; Your timing is perfect. Help me remember when I grow despondent that eternity for me will come in Your time, and that I need not worry. Help me remember that You have given me eternal life through Jesus Christ Your Son.

To God be the glory

42. Factory Tour

Always loved factory tours…
The gears and cogs meshing
Round and round
Pushing bottles of soda pop
On their stuttering journey to be capped.

Chains and pulleys
Moving up and down
Placing car doors exactly on the frames
With a satisfying ker-CLUNK.

And snaky conveyor belts
Sliding bars of chocolate to the cutting blade
And then catching them below
To slide on to boxing.

Once I was in a pretzel factory.
We watched the dough come out the tubes
And begin to wrap around the pegs
That twisted them into little prayer arms.
The tour guide told us the story
Of the monk who made these
As a reminder to pray…
As a reminder of intertwined love.
The little twists moved on
to a boiling bath.

And as each plopped into the steamy pot,
I wrapped my arms around myself...
My little prayer wings to keep me safe
While the wheels and gears and chains and blades
Whirled round and round...
Ceaseless grinding and pounding and tapping
To make this...
And this...
Into that.

===

 But all things should be done decently and in order.
1 Corinthians 14:40

For by Him all things were created, in heaven and on earth, visible and invisible, whether thrones or dominions or rulers or authorities—all things were created through Him and for Him. And He is before all things, and in Him all things hold together.
Colossians 1:16-17

For His invisible attributes, namely, His eternal power and divine nature, have been clearly perceived, ever since the creation of the world, in the things that have been made. So they are without excuse.
Romans 1:20

Meanderings: Even the pretzels remind us to pray! What items call you to prayer? How can God use you to make something new? To continue His orderliness? How does God's orderliness influence your prayers?

Father, all around me I see evidence of Your orderliness. All things hold together in You. The world is filled with Your creation and is not abstract nor haphazard. Open my eyes to what You have done! Help me see the exquisite patterns in the skies, in the earth, and indeed in our very bodies. And help me to understand that these show Your glory.

To God be the glory

43. Just A Moment (Pompeii)

"Hand me the needle."
"Just a moment."
"How about a kiss?"
"Just a moment"
"Come give Daddy a hug."
"Just a moment."
"It's time to let the dog out."
"Just a moment."
"Quick! Take it out of the oven!"
"Just a moment."
"Look at the sky!"
"Just a moment."

And in that moment…
She began to hand over the needle
He leaned in for a kiss
Little hands reached for Daddy
The dog went to the gate
The bread burned
And the sky was black with sudden ash

In that moment.
Breathing stopped
In that moment.
Voices failed
In that moment.

Arms were frozen
In that moment.
In that moment, life ceased…

And in another moment, long after,
We discovered their lives again…
Saw the grimaces,
The final jerking movements,
The writhe of the dog,
The clay baking pan shattered,
The needle…
Such a moment…
When time had a seizure
And stopped.

===

 *So teach us to number our days that we may
get a heart of wisdom.
Psalm 90:12*

*The heart of man plans his way, but the Lord establishes
his steps.
Proverbs 16:9*

*Come now, you who say, "Today or tomorrow we will go
into such and such a town and spend a year there and
trade and make a profit"— yet you do not know what
tomorrow will bring. What is your life? For you are a
mist that appears for a little time and then vanishes.*

Instead you ought to say, "If the Lord wills, we will live and do this or that."
James 4:13-15

Meanderings: Has there been a time when you put off doing or saying something... and then regretted it? How can you be more mindful of your moments and days? What is the value of an hour?

Father, our lives are in Your hands. Our moments are in Your hands. You count our days and years. It is difficult to fathom life being over in a second, when I expected to go on for much more time. I am not in control. Father, that is hard to wrap my brain around. Help me accept Your time, and to be ready for Your time.

To God be the glory

44. Reluctant Weaver

They hum as they weave…
The old songs of women working…
Four notes,
Five notes,
Over and over in a faint chant.

Threads pass between their fingers
Four strands,
Five strands,
Over and over in an unending pattern of time past.

If I dare gaze with longing beyond the mountains,
If I dare sigh,
Then the women stop,
Threads drop,
Humming ceases.
No word arrows pierce me,
But eye arrows go deep into my soul.

They know. They know
My dreams
And they know. They know
That I am here only in my body
And they know. They know
That I am not woven into their fabric
And they know. They know
That I cannot hum the old notes,

And that I sit awkwardly at the end
With different colored threads
Woven outside the lines.

==

 *Do not be conformed to this world, but be
transformed by the renewal of your mind, that
by testing you may discern what is the will of
God, what is good and acceptable and perfect.*
Romans 12:2

*If you were of the world, the world would love you as its
own; but because you are not of the world, but I chose
you out of the world, therefore the world hates you.*
John 15:19

*To all who are in Rome, beloved of God, called to be
saints: Grace to you and peace from God our Father and
the Lord Jesus Christ.*
Romans 1:7

Meanderings: Have you ever felt as if
you are out of step with others around
you? That you march to the beat of a
different drummer? How difficult is it
for you to take a stand even when you
stand alone? What happens when you

are called to be a saint in an environment where others are not understanding?

Father, I know what it is like to be different, to not fit in, to not be what others expect. I have struggled with not being accepted, and being looked at with distain. Yet, You have called me to be set apart, to be Your saint. You have called me to a different standard than that of the world. I ask that You equip me for the life to which You have called me.

To God be the glory

45. Rows

Rows in my hair...
Rows in my clothes...
Rows on my cheeks and under my eyes.
And the rows stretch on...

O Mama...
On to the shadows...
Red dirt on my toes as I pick the bolls
In the rows.

Walking those rows
Toward sunset,
Not looking back...
Tossing my basket...
Dropping my hoe.
Treading those rows
Swirling red dust

"Sweet Mama!
I'm coming!
I'm coming home!"
Pounding those rows,
Just want to go home.
Lord, just want to go home.

And the darkness gathers,
Rows fade and dissolve.

And I'm tired, Mama,
Staring at rows.
Just want to go home.
Away from the rows.
Home.
Rows.

(Published in *The Ekphrastic Review,* March 2021)

===

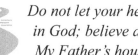 *Do not let your hearts be troubled. You believe
in God; believe also in Me.
My Father's house has many rooms; if that
were not so, would I have told you that I am
going there to prepare a place for you?
John 14: 1-2*

*For we know that if the earthly tent we live in is
destroyed, we have a building from God, an eternal
house in heaven, not built by human hands.
Meanwhile we groan, longing to be clothed instead with
our heavenly dwelling, because when we are clothed, we
will not be found naked.   For while we are in this tent,
we groan and are burdened, because we do not wish to
be unclothed but to be clothed instead with our heavenly
dwelling, so that what is mortal may be swallowed up by
life.
2 Corinthians 5:1-5*

Meanderings: What is "home" for you? Do you look forward to the day when you are home with your Father? Do any physical elements of your earthly home take on spiritual meaning?

Father, going home!! O that wonderful day to be in Your presence! Life here is precious and I have been privileged with life. I will not rush Your perfect timing. But... I long for Heaven, to see Your face, to be with You forever. Meanwhile, please give me grace, wisdom, discernment as I dwell here.

To God be the glory

46. He Shattered My Box

My God doesn't live in a box.
A grave could not hold Him.
My God can spill blood
And still live.

My God can take pain,
and mold it into beauty.
My God can step on water,
Tread the snake head,
Command the wind.

Even government officials
Were astounded.
Religious people
Harbored jealousy.

But you and I,
Commoners really,
Delighted in His coming…
And His overcoming.

My God shattered the box
Of my past
Into dust and tiny shards.
My God knew my name…
And still invited me to follow.

I don't fall prostrate
On cold stone to kiss His grave.
He is not there.
My God…

(Published in *The Ekphrastic Review* April 2021)
==

 I know that You can do all things,
  And that no purpose of Yours can be thwarted.
  Job 42:2

  For nothing will be impossible with God."
Luke 1:37

There is none like You, O Lord;
You are great, and great is Your name in might.
Jeremiah 10:6

Meanderings: He Who holds the
universe knows Your name! How do
you feel and react when you ponder
how powerful He is, and how He knows
you? Are you ever guilty of trying to
put God into a box?

Father, Your power overwhelms me. I am awed by all You can do…. far beyond the bounds of nature. You are not contained or constrained, for it is all under Your dominion. When I am puny, remind me that You are in control, and that You have mighty power. I praise You, for there is none like You, and yet… You know my name.

To God be the glory

47. Basket of Fruit

I placed all the fruit into the basket,
The one meant to be carried on my head. But
I carried it on my back, instead, and
It pulled me backwards to the ground.

Fruit began to roll down the hill, and
I scrambled to catch them.
Fruit in the basket,
I carried it in my arms, and
It pitched me forward.

Fruit tumbled down the hill, and
I grabbed them, bruising some.
Fruit in the basket,
Basket on the head.

I finished the journey, and
Stepped onto the porch.
Mashed fruit in the basket,
basket on the bench, with
juicy stickiness
dripping down my neck and
oozing through my hair, and
juice puddling on the bench.

The flies were already gathering.

The LORD is the One Who will go before you. He will be with you; He will not leave you or abandon you. Do not be afraid or discouraged.
Deuteronomy 31: 8

Do not fear, for I am with you; do not be afraid, for I am your God. I will strengthen you; I will help you; I will hold on to you with My righteous right hand.
Isaiah 41: 10

Don't worry about anything, but in everything, through prayer and petition with thanksgiving, present your requests to God. And the peace of God, which surpasses all understanding, will guard your hearts and minds in Christ Jesus.
Philippians 4:6-7

Meanderings: On this life path, you will bear burdens as you walk. It may look as if all you did ended in disaster. How long does it take you to carry the basket the right way? How do you find the encouragement to keep on keeping on?

Father, I try... and I fail. I grow discouraged too easily and give up. I worry. I need You, O, I need You. When I fall, make mistakes, disobey... I need You. Help me understand the truth of how You go before me, how You hold me. Help me finish the journey even if messy, for I know that You are my God.

To God be the glory

48. Emilie

O Emilie…
I never knew your pain.
If I had known, I would have crawled into your skin,
And shared the silent weight.
I would have beat against the darkness
That was hovering over you.

When your baby tummy ached,
You grimaced your little mouth,
Screamed and whimpered.
I would rub your belly…
Pat your back…
Jiggle you close to my heart.
And when the pain eased,
You relaxed in my arms,
Closed your eyes,
Peacefully slept.

Now I stand by your bed.
One hand covers my mouth
Trying to stifle the anguish
forming deep in my throat.
One arm is around my belly,
fist clenched.

You lie there, not moving, eyes closed.
Your body looks relaxed, peaceful.

Yet your mouth hangs open in a silent whimper.
I want to scream at you: "Wake up! Wake up!"
I want to hold you… again… close to my heart.

Emilie.
I wish you could know this.
Your pain did not come to a close;
It simply transferred.
Now I carry the weight in the lingering darkness.

(Dedicated to Danielle Swofford, in memory of Emilie)

==

 Weeping may tarry for the night, but joy comes with the morning.
Psalm 30: 5

"Blessed are those who mourn, for they shall be comforted.
Matthew 5:4

Casting all your anxieties on Him, because He cares for you.   1 Peter 5:7

Meanderings: Is there a memory of a painful experience that Satan wants to use against you? That he wants to use to destroy you? How do you rebuke him? How do you find the strength to take the next step? How do you learn to use the pain and sorrow of the past to make a difference in the future?

Father, sorrow eats at my soul and I need You for Your perfect comfort. I do not understand. I cannot understand, in my human imperfection, how this all works. All I can do is trust You. And that's hard when my heart is broken, and my world has turned dark. Help me lean on Your promise that joy will come again. That I shall find Your comfort. That You care for me.

To God be the glory

49. Why Can't We Just All Gather Around the Cake Again?
(A Black and White Photo)

Eight girls in pajamas
Sitting in a circle on the floor
Around Vicki and her birthday cake.

We had been singing,
waiting for her to blow out the candles.

Kathy-with-a-K had her hair in rollers.
The rest of us would follow later.

We chattered
Teachers, boys, colleges, prom.

Our biggest trauma: JFK in Dallas.
We had no idea that Bobby and MLK were next.

Vicki blew out 16 candles;
Debbie coughed in the smoke and
Ruthie and Linda clapped their hands.
Dianne began chanting:
HOWMANYCANDLESDOESITTAKE...
Cathy-with-a-C joined in:
TOLIGHTVICKI'SBIRTHDAYCAKE

Then we giggled.
So childish… candles and singing…
We loved it.

College came true.   So did certain boys.
So did 911.

Cathy-with-a-C disappeared. Ruthie died.
Linda moved to Europe.
Vicki's husband died. So did Debbie's… in Nam.
Kathy-with-a-K had cancer.
Dianne had eight kids.

I stare at the old photo.   We didn't know.
We couldn't know that life was just about
To get as hazy as candle smoke.

(Dedicated to Sherry, Judy, Marianne, Nikki, Sue, Carole, Peggy, Karen, Betty)

==

 Brothers, I do not consider that I have made it my own. But one thing I do: forgetting what lies behind and straining forward to what lies ahead.
Philippians 3:13

Therefore if any man be in Christ, he is a new creature: old things are passed away; behold, all things are become new.
2 Corinthians 5:17

Even though I walk through the valley of the shadow of death, I will fear no evil, for You are with me; Your rod and Your staff, they comfort me.
Psalm 23:4

Meanderings: Has life gone the way you thought it would? Were there disappointments, sorrows, and joys that you could not expect? Looking back, can you see how the Lord was your guide as you continued forward?

Father, while the past will always be a part of my memories, I thank You for how You brought me into the present... that I don't have to live in the past. I thank You for those in my past, and how You protected us and brought us forward. I went through many valleys, and looking back, I praise You for being there with me, even when I did not realize it.

To God be the glory

50. Pain

I. You pounce from the dark,
Clawing and gnawing,
Seeking to devour.
You steal sleep by night,
And alertness by day.
You interrupt life flow…
Even my sentences become fragments
And my words become strangled utterances.
Your sudden savagery staggers me.
I reel, groaning and crying.
Pain!
You will not win this battle.
I will stand again and fight.

II. Like being in a small room
with no windows…
No doors.
No way of escape.
no place to hide.

A man with a club is in the room with me.
He strikes my ear
And I cringe and fall to the floor,
Crying and holding my ear.
I know that he has the ability to hit even harder,
But this blow is hard enough.

I crouch, tense myself in readiness for the next strike.
There is no rhythm to his abuse.
Perhaps ten or twelve hits in a row…
Then none.
Then two.
Then a blessed time with nothing.
Then more.
Nothing gives escape.
I can only wait for the man to grow weak
And die.
===

Praise be to the God and Father of our Lord Jesus Christ, the Father of compassion and the God of all comfort, Who comforts us in all our troubles, so that we can comfort those in any trouble with the comfort we ourselves receive from God.
2 Corinthians 1: 3-8

Not only that, but we rejoice in our sufferings, knowing that suffering produces endurance, and endurance produces character, and character produces hope, and hope does not put us to shame, because God's love has been poured into our hearts through the Holy Spirit Who has been given to us.
Romans 5:3-5

You have kept count of my tossings; put my tears in Your bottle. Are they not in Your book?
Psalm 56:8

Meanderings: How is pain necessary? What is a time that you had to deal with pain? How did you react to the pain? How can you rejoice in your pain?

Father, I am not always appreciative of the pain in my life. Only later, do I calm down and see You holding me through the valley of pain. Help me to handle pain in the best ways possible… to look for You in the midst. And while I hate pain, I ask that You help me appreciate the lessons found in times of pain.

To God be the glory

51. O God...

I'm tired of hurting… of waking every day in pain.
I want to be a normal teen again… Can I? Please?
I feel cursed… waiting for answers.

I am sorry. I sound selfish. I feel like a burden.
Some days, I just want to give up.
But God is a miracle worker… so powerful… my God!!
My One and Only!

I praise You for my life, even though
I have no understanding of Your ways.
You are with me;
You know how I feel.

But I am worn out. Tired. Weak.
Someday I will be in no pain.
O, my God!

(Written by Maddi Parson)

==

 *The LORD is close to the brokenhearted and
saves those who are crushed in spirit.
Psalm 34:18*

I will say of the LORD, "He is my refuge and my fortress, my God, in whom I trust."
Psalm 91: 2

The night racks my bones, and the pain that gnaws me takes no rest.
Job 30:17

Meanderings: When bad happens to you, it may make no sense. Does it make you tired and ready to give up? How do you call out to God?

Father, it is during these times that I just must hand it over to You. It takes faith, Lord, and sometimes I feel that my faith is small... inadequate. Help me just look to You, even when I don't understand. Help me take one step at a time. Help me praise You, no matter what.

To God be the glory

52. And I Don't Know Her Name

I don't know her name.
We meet often at this junction.
She comes from the east;
I come from the north.

I carry my shopping bag
For my trip to market in the south.
I don't know her destination.
She carries a small bag
And a book.

I don't know her name.
But we nod in recognition.
Once we spoke,
A non-committing "Good morning."

She seems much older;
Her voice is low and crackles.
She walks slowly,
Slightly bent,
With her plain coat
Dragging in the puddles.

I don't know her name.
She is intriguing…
So different…
In that I-have-a-story way.

I long to say more…
To ask more…
But she has a private dignity
That closes my mouth.

And so we pass.
And so we nod.
And so we murmur "Good morning."
And so I don't yet know her name.

==

 *Do not neglect to show hospitality to strangers,
for thereby some have entertained angels
unawares.
Hebrews 13:2*

*For the whole law is fulfilled in one word: "You shall
love your neighbor as yourself."
Galatians 5:14*

*Show hospitality to one another without grumbling.
1 Peter 4:9*

Meanderings: Is it difficult for you to make friends? To extend hospitality? Do you speak with kindness to the anonymous people in your life, such as the check out clerk, the mailman, the one stocking shelves, the one you meet daily on the job?

Father, help me to be more hospitable and kind to others. Give me the sensibility to avoid danger, while also extending a smile. Help me compliment someone who might not be recognized. I praise You for loving me. Now I need Your guidance in loving others.

To God be the glory

53. Still… the Magic

Let old memories die hard,
Let them linger even as I fade.
Let them enter my heart with no announcement.
Let them visit my soul with soothing magic.

Swimming among the lilies…
Friends…
My love…

I remember our hair floating on the water,
The songs of tiny frogs,
The flowers in our waves.

I remember how he chose me…
Even while I can no longer recall his name.
I remember my fingers in his black curls…
Even while I can no longer remember his face.
I remember how I trembled... was it my mouth…
my hands?
Was it his touch?

Was there silence? Laughter?
Did he call my name?
I no longer know.

Memories have frayed edges; image melts into image.
Words continue to elude me,
While the tatters of what was still come.
Perhaps… that is the magic.

==

Finally, brothers, whatever is true, whatever is honorable, whatever is just, whatever is pure, whatever is lovely, whatever is commendable, if there is any excellence, if there is anything worthy of praise, think about these things.
Philippians 4:8

I will give thanks to the Lord with my whole heart; I will recount all of Your wonderful deeds.
Psalm 9:1

Meanderings: It happens. Memories fade, sometimes into dementia, sometimes just a lost name. When do you lose a memory? How do you trigger the memory to return? How do you treat others who cannot remember? How do you give comfort to him or her?

Father, precious memories, how they linger. Thank You for the capacity to remember and help me to never take this lightly. Help me remember others who have impacted my life. Help me give praise for the memories that are true and just.   And help me to help others who struggle with memory.   Fill my mouth with the words that are just right to console them.

To God be the glory

54. Being Eleven

Should I smile? Or not?
If I smile, do I show teeth?
Should I wave?
A tiny twinkling of fingers?
A queenly gesture?

If I look at her, she'll think I'm stupid
But if I look the other way,
Then I'm a loser.

Do I look back at him?
Too forward?
If he looks at me, do I hold his gaze?
Or look down? Or off to the horizon?

If I get three steps closer,
I'll ask her name.
Maybe two steps.
Maybe just go the other way.

Is my shirt too tight?
Are these the right shoes?
Does he like mauve?

Girls are weird. I wish this was just
black and white.

Boys are so dumb. They just don't get
all the shades of gray.

She's looking.
Do I say "hi"? Wave?
I'm stupid.

My hair is crazy. I should have pulled it back in a pony.

My hair is crazy. I should just shave it all.

Maybe I'll just say "Oh, hi."

Maybe I'll just bump into her and say, "Excuse me."
Maybe…

"Excuse me."

"Oh, hi."

Now what?

Now what?

(Dedicated to Bradden Parson, with memories of being 11)

==

The fear of man lays a snare,
but whoever trusts in the Lord is safe.
Proverbs 29: 25

Then Moses said to the Lord, "Please, Lord, I have never
been eloquent, neither recently nor in time past, nor
since You have spoken to Your servant; for I am slow of
speech and slow of tongue.
Exodus 4:10-15

Let no one look down on your youthfulness, but rather in
speech, conduct, love, faith and purity, show yourself as
an example.
1 Timothy 4:12

Then I said, "Alas, Lord God!
Behold, I do not know how to speak,
Because I am a youth."
Jeremiah 1:6

Meanderings: Shyness and excuses are
a kind of fear. Do you speak to others
freely and naturally about the Lord, or
do shyness and excuses hinder you?
When was the last time you explained
Scripture to someone?

Father, So often I let fear get between me and others, especially when I want to invite them to follow Jesus, or to talk about spiritual matters. Help me remember that neither age, handicaps, education nor status matter when we are compelled to speak of You. Thank You for the times You have helped me overcome my fear.

To God be the glory

55. A Chocolate Love Story

I roll over in bed and see his
charcoal silvery waves
sticking straight up.

If I pat them down, he'll awake.

Fifty years ago, I ran my fingers through his
dark chocolate curls…
so delicious.

And then the curls became short
for the job interview.

And then shorter… a wasteland…
for Vietnam.

And then in the photo with the baby,
curls frame his face again,
and the baby has ringlets.

Now…
a small pink spot tops the silvery waves,
and the charcoal… no longer chocolate… hides beneath.
I reach across the pillow
to run my fingers along his head,
trace the lines of the phantom curls.

Looking back, I loved
his hair…
loved him.

Looking forward, I love
his hair…
love him.

Awake, my chocolate love. Awake.

===

 *Then the Lord God said, "It is not good that
the man should be alone; I will make him a
helper fit for him."*
Genesis 2:18

*Above all, keep loving one another earnestly, since love
covers a multitude of sins.*
1 Peter 4:8

*What therefore God has joined together, let not man
separate.   Mark 10:9*

Meanderings: What do you love most
about your spouse? How did God join
you together?   How does He keep you
together? Does love grow sweeter as
time goes on?

Father, I praise you for my husband!   You knew exactly what I needed, and You provided!   Thank You for the love You give through him.   Forgive me when I become thoughtless or careless in my love for him, and equip me to continue loving for time to come.   Thank You for showing me that aging love is precious.

To God be the glory

56. Great Grandmother

Like an antique lamp,
Valuable.
Beautiful.
Faded.
Old.

Her colors shine like light;
When she tells her stories,
She lights up the room.

(Written by Luke Parson)

===

57. Great Grandfather

He is like an old book,
Broken back,
Crumbling pages,
Torn corners.

Still, his gold lettering
On fine leather
Shows like a light in darkness.
His pages have the stories of the past.

(Written by Luke Parson)

===

58. My Family

My family is a lizard.
The backbone, Father,
Keeping us strong.

The little feet, Mother,
Pit-patting busily
Getting things done.

And I?   I am the little tail
That will break off and make
A family of my own.

(Written by Luke Parson. Published in *The Messenger* . Published in *Missouri Youth Write*)

===

 Honor your father and your mother, so that you may live long in the land the Lord your God is giving you.
Exodus 20: 12

Children are a heritage from the LORD, offspring a reward from Him.
Psalm 127: 3

Children, obey your parents in everything, for this pleases the Lord.
Colossians 3: 20

Fathers, do not exasperate your children; instead, bring them up in the training and instruction of the Lord.
Ephesians 6: 4

These commandments that I give you today are to be on your hearts. Impress them on your children. Talk about them when you sit at home and when you walk along the road, when you lie down and when you get up.
Deuteronomy 6: 6-7

Children's children are a crown to the aged, and parents are the pride of their children.
Proverbs 17:6

I am reminded of your sincere faith, which first lived in your grandmother Lois and in your mother Eunice and, I am persuaded, now lives in you also.
1 Timothy 1:5

But from everlasting to everlasting the Lord's love is with those who fear Him, and His righteousness with their children's children.
Psalm 103:17

One generation commends Your works to another; they
tell of Your mighty acts.
Psalm 145:4

Meanderings: Do you have memories
of grandparents, or perhaps great
grandparents? How did they impact
your life? How did your parents show
you God's love and plans for your
life? How are you passing on a
testimony of God to your children
and grandchildren?

Father, family is so important to me. I thank You that
You placed me in a family that feared God, that
worshipped You, that took Your word seriously, and that
passed it on to me. I thank You for three generations
ahead of me that never faltered in their faith, and
showed me how to persevere. I am grateful for my son
and his children… and their children. When I consider
how You have allowed me to know seven generations, I
am humbled… and amazed. Help me to love them as
You loved me… sacrificially.

To God be the glory

59. Patience

Patience is what I lack.
I get off track
When I have to wait.
Nothing more that I hate.
Patience…

(Written by Luke Parson)

===

60. My Heart

My heart is like a leather coat.
Warm, like a fire on a cold night.
Soft, like a bed of feathers.
It can be torn…
And I can share it.

(Written by Luke Parson)

===

But the Lord said to Samuel, "Do not look on his appearance or on the height of his stature, because I have rejected him. For the Lord sees not as man sees: man looks on the outward appearance, but the Lord looks on the heart."
1 Samuel 16:7

As in water face reflects face, so the heart of man reflects the man.
Proverbs 27:19

For I do not understand my own actions. For I do not do what I want, but I do the very thing I hate.
Romans 7: 15

Keep your heart with all vigilance, for from it flow the springs of life. Proverbs 4:23

A good name is to be chosen rather than great riches.
Proverbs 22: 1

Meanderings: Do you look at yourself honestly? Try to see yourself as others see you? Do you consider how God sees you? Does God know your heart? Does He know your strength and flaws? Reflect on how He still loves you... despite every flaw. Reflect on how He knows your name, and that you are fearfully and wonderfully created for His purpose.

Father, You have created not only our bodies, but also our personalities, our souls, minds, and hearts. Forgive me when I fail to use what You have endowed me with, and give me strength to do Your will. Help me guard my heart. Help me be that "leather coat" to others.

To God be the glory

61. The Creek

Down the hill,
Behind the barn,
And past the pond,
The creek lies tangled in the willow grove.

Like an S following S,
It slithers,
Slips,
Swirls,
From the coming-in-place
To who-knows-where:

The Atlantic Ocean, maybe,
Or the Mississip',
Or Tom Glenn's dammed up lake.

I don't know where it goes;
It wanders…
Out of my sight…

(published in *Synapse*, 1970)

===

But let justice roll on like a river, righteousness
like a never-failing stream!
Amos 5: 24

He makes me lie down in green pastures, He leads me beside quiet waters.
Psalm 23: 2

Whoever believes in Me, as the Scripture has said, 'Out of his heart will flow rivers of living water.'"
John 7:38

Then the angel showed me the river of the water of life, bright as crystal, flowing from the throne of God and of the Lamb.
Revelation 22:1

The earth was without form and void, and darkness was over the face of the deep. And the Spirit of God was hovering over the face of the waters.
Genesis 1:2

Meanderings: Water is used in Scripture for so many functions. Can you list some of the uses of water in the Word? Why do you think that water was chosen as the symbol so many times? How do you identify with the Scriptural use of water?

Father, from creation to eternity, water has played such a huge role in the faith journey. Born of water, baptized in water, washed with water, drinking the living water.... Father, I thirst for You! When I see rivers, remind me of Your power, and Your desire for me to come before You... clean and washed. Wash me, and I shall be whiter than snow.

To God be the glory

62. Steam

Where does steam go
When its seen no more?
Where does it go?
Where does it soar?

Does it go above
And build a steam home
Or a steam castle
In Steam-City Rome?

Or does it float away?
Does it make the clouds?
Or is it the wind,
Blustery and loud?

Or maybe the steam
Just dies away,
Never comes back
In any way.

(Written in 8th grade)

===

 When He utters His voice, there is a tumult of waters in the heavens,
And He causes the clouds to ascend from the end of the earth;

He makes lightning for the rain,
And brings out the wind from His storehouses
Jeremiah 10:13

You, indeed, have made my days short in length, and my
life span as nothing in Your sight. Yes, every mortal man
is only a vapor.
Psalm 39:5

People are like a vapor, their days like a shadow that
disappears.
Psalm 144:4

All that is done without God's guidance is vanity: futile,
meaningless—a wisp of smoke, a vapor that vanishes,
merely chasing the wind.
Ecclesiastics 1:2

Meanderings: Steam vapor is seen
briefly and then it disappears. How is
this a good analogy for life?

Father, I desire that my life count for You. Even though
my days are few, they are for a purpose. Do not let me
be like steam vapor which simply exists and then is gone.
Let me use my time to share the gospel, to love others, to
be true to Your Word.

To God be the glory

63. The Struggle

...of birth,
A body fighting to leave
All that was warm
And dark
And protected.

...like a chick pecking
Its way through
The shell....

...like a soul
And body
Releasing
...at death.

==

 For none of us lives to himself, and none of us dies to himself. For if we live, we live to the Lord, and if we die, we die to the Lord. So then, whether we live or whether we die, we are the Lord's.
Romans 14:7-9

Yes, we are of good courage, and we would rather be away from the body and at home with the Lord.
2 Corinthians 5:8

When a woman is giving birth, she has sorrow because her hour has come, but when she has delivered the baby, she no longer remembers the anguish, for joy that a human being has been born into the world.
John 16:21

Meanderings: Imagine the struggles of birth for both the mother and the baby. What words come to mind? Is the life after those struggles worth it? Then imagine the struggles of death. Consider the life after death.

Father, the struggle is real! I pray for each person who is intensely struggling with life and death. While I desire the promised eternal life, I still struggle with life on earth, and carrying out my appointed purpose. I want to pass on the good news of Jesus, even while desiring heavenly life with You. How difficult it must be for some who who don't know You, and struggle to hold on to the only life they know. I pray for them to come to a personal relationship with You.

To God be the glory

64. October 25... Nate

Splashing sunshine
Covered the city,
Tracing gold rims on
The Greek Orthodox Church domes.

We could see the domes
From the hospital room,
Framed by vibrant fall leaves.

Our once vibrant Nate
Lay framed by
Hoses and needles
And machines that
Clicked and hummed.

Before, he was like those dancing leaves,
Moving and teasing and laughing.

Now...
As the machines ceased,
We watched his fingers
Become blue... then gray,
Shadows of who he was.
We knew his soul
Had gone beyond the sunshine.

We knew he was in
Brighter light than ever,
Even as the light in our hearts
Dimmed.

(Dedicated to Sherelyn and Jim Hornick, in memory of Nate)

===

 Your sun will no longer set, Nor will your moon wane; For you will have the Lord for an everlasting light, And the days of your mourning will be over.
Isaiah 60:20

Let everything that has breath praise the LORD. Praise ye the LORD.
Psalm 150:6

Meanderings: Watching someone die: sorrow, fear, relief, pain... and joy? What words come to mind about the death of a loved one? How can there be joy in death? How can that joy be healing to our grief?

Father, Nate was a gift to us. And we praise You, even in our grief. From the beginning of his life to the end, from the rising of the sun to the setting, we praise You. Please give us the peace, the understanding that his life was not in vain. Please banish the shadows of mourning. We thank You for allowing us to share in his life for those few short years.

To God be the glory

65. To My Friend

Your shoulder…. My shoulder…
We leave damp cloth
As we cry our sorrows.

Your laugh…. My laugh…
Joy lingers, hanging
In the silence between us.

Your arm…. My arm…
We link, elbow to elbow
As we stroll and talk.

Your eyes…. My eyes…
Our gaze meets
With wicked winks.

Your heart…. My heart…
Our understandings
Are deep and old.
Such it is with my friend.

(Dedicated to Debbie Pollard)

==

If either of them falls down, one can help the other up. But pity anyone who falls and has no one to help them up.
Ecclesiastics 4: 10

Perfume and incense bring joy to the heart, and the pleasantness of a friend springs from their heartfelt advice.
Proverbs 27:9

Wounds from a friend can be trusted, but an enemy multiplies kisses.
Proverbs 27: 6

Greater love has no one than this: to lay down one's life for one's friends.
John 15:13

Meanderings: Who are your closest friends? Do they speak to you honestly? Do they desire the best for you? Do they know the worst about you and still love you? What do you look for in a friend?

Father, You have placed the most remarkable people in my life, and I am privileged to call them friends. Thank You for how You picked them so carefully. Thank You for how we are there for each other, despite time and miles. You have blessed me with these who know me inside and out.

To God be the glory

66. Brother: A First Glance

When I was two, I crawled up on the chair,
And then onto the table
To see this baby…
This doll that was not like
My other dolls…
This doll whose eyes moved,
But were mostly closed.
This doll whose mouth opened
To cry.
This doll with warm skin.

I loved you,
Wanted to hold you
And pat your head,
And feed you.
I wanted to put my other doll beside you
And share all that I had.
I did not yet know how to say
That I shared my heart.

(Dedicated to Darrell Newquist)

===

 *Keep on loving one another as brothers and
sisters.
Hebrews 13:1*

Anyone who loves God must also love their brother and sister.
1 John 4: 21

Meanderings: What are some first memories of your siblings? How did you show love to them, or how did they show love to you? Did your relationship change?

Father, I thank You for my siblings, and for this first one, my brother. While we struggled at times, I praise You that we came out of childhood as good friends. Help me be the good big sister that You intended me to be.

To God be the glory

67. When Simon Comes Marching Home

When April winds blew high, lifting spirits and soaring kites, Miriam put away her flute and reached for her hoe. When April came, Miriam folded her knitting and put on her planting apron. When April came, as all Aprils eventually do, she nourished again the hope that Simon would return.

He left on an April day such as this, with the breeze tossing his light brown hair across his forehead, and he, marching jauntily on, never looking back until he reached the main road, and then, turning only briefly and waving his hand high before he disappeared at the curve. It was only fitting that he would return on such a day.

Miriam leaned on her hoe and tightly forced her eyes shut, trying to remember Simon's face. He was handsome; she was sure of that, for he had his father's broad generous features. He had the same gray eyes, so sober one moment, so happy the next, the same patrician nose, the same easy smile. Simon's father was the most handsome man Miriam ever knew, and when he died, she was grateful for his son, who grew every day to look more like the father he had adored.

"Mother?"

Miriam came back to the earthy reality. Sarah was barefoot, twisting her toes into the loamy soil, and searching her mother's eyes.

"Mother?"

"You shouldn't be out here without your shoes, dear."

Sarah ignored her mother's remark. "It is 5:00. What are you doing out here?"

Miriam raised her arms and spread her fingers wide. "Look, Sarah."

She indicated the rising sun, stretching its pink fingers across the silvery sky, ready to flick away the last flecks of night. "It is April now, and Simon will be coming home!"

She dropped the hoe, and with stained arthritic hands, she grasped Sarah's plump wrists. "Simon is coming home! And he will say, 'Where is the garden? How are my sheep? Have you planted the wheat?' We must not disappoint him, Sarah; he has been gone so long. We must be ready for him."

Sarah tested her wrists against her mother's grip, but the older woman held fast. "Mother," she murmured, "Mother, no, don't say this."

Miriam did not hear the plea. "I will say, 'Simon, you are tired. Sit, and I will fix tea, and we will talk.' I have so much to ask him: Where have you been? Were they good to you? What did you do?" Miriam laughed suddenly and lightly.

"But if I know Simon, he will insist that he is not tired. He will want to see everything right away, and of course, I will let him. He could talk me into anything, Sarah. Anything."

Miriam released Sarah and stiffly knelt to retrieve the fallen hoe. Sarah remained mute, with her arms outstretched still, and the breezes blowing her hair about her neck and wrapping her gown about her ankles.

Miriam looked up. "Child, you'll catch cold standing on this damp ground. Run in. We have much to do today."

Sarah remembered with painful acuity that day last September when they came to tell them about Simon. She was sweeping the front room; her mother was working in the back room. They came down the lane, straight to the open door, and Sarah watched their faces and feet keep time. Their pedantic cadence mesmerized her as she found herself moving toward the door to greet the visitors. Guests were rare and each one made a special day.

The tallest man returned Sarah's greeting and asked to meet her mother. Miriam came from the back room, smiling, and bidding the guests to be seated.

"No, thanks, Mam," said the tall man. "We, we, can't stay long. You see, we came to deliver a message."

A message? Messages were as rare as guests, but never as welcome. Messages meant only bad news and Miriam searched each man's face for the fatal clue.

"Mam." The tall man cleared his throat. "Mam, I don't know how to tell you this. Believe me, Mam, I don't want to say this, but when it's gotta be done, it's gotta be done. You know."

Miriam stared with uncomprehending eyes. No, she didn't know.

"Simon, Mam, your son, uh, he was wounded, you see, and uh, he was brave, Mam, brave to the very end, but they couldn't help him none, you know. He was wounded, Mam, and they couldn't do nothing for him, but he was brave, Mam. He was a real brave boy."

That was in September, and chill that drove the leaves from their high perches, and the snow which drove the chill deep into the earth did not move Miriam. There was chill in Sarah's heart, but she did not know if Miriam felt it or not.

"Simon," Miriam said. "Simon could get every acorn in these hills before the squirrels even thought about them."

Again, "Sarah, we must oil these runners. Simon may want to use the sled." And again, "Simon is 23 today." Sarah cried that night. Last week she had become 18, and no one mentioned it.

Now it was April, and the birds returned from the south, and sap returned from the roots, and Miriam returned to the garden to cultivate and hover over the plants that responded to her need for living, growing things.

Now it was April, and Miriam rocked on the porch in the gathering twilight, her head following each movement of the chair until her chin dropped onto her chest. Then, with utter bone-weariness, she sighed .

"Everything is returning," she said, "but I don't think Simon will return tonight. It's dark. I don't think he will be traveling now."

Sarah was taking quick, deft stitches beside the lamp, but put aside her needle. She took Miriam's hand and led her from the porch. "Tomorrow, Mother, maybe tomorrow."

And the flickering lamp hid the tear that coursed down each woman's cheek.

===

And now, O Lord, for what do I wait? My hope is in You.
Psalm 39:7

Know that wisdom is such to your soul; if you find it, there will be a future, and your hope will not be cut off.
Proverbs 24:14

Meanderings: Miriam has a hope, but it is not based in reality. Sarah is in reality, but not in hope. Is there wisdom in Miriam's hope? How can she find a future and a hope? How can Sarah find the same? Have you ever found yourself in the position of either Miriam or Sarah? How did faith help you?

Father, so, so very difficult to live without hope. And yet to live in a false hope seems worse. Help me face reality and develop a hope based on wisdom... a hope based on You. Help me wait on You: on Your perfect times and ways as I search for the answers, as I search for hope.

To God be the glory

68. You Know You Are a Mostly Normal Woman WHEN...

1. You water the fern with old gritty ice cubes that fall to the bottom of the freezer.
2. You bounce on the bed after checking that everyone is out of the house.
3. You stash fluid pills ;and chocolate side by side in your desk drawer.
4. You pray your college son will call, and then dread hearing the phone ring.
5. Your interior decorating means arranging the furniture around the carpet stains.
6. You petition the city government to crop spray prozac.
7. You open a new can of coffee, plunge in your nose, and take a deep breath... just to get jump started.
8. You celebrate and shout, "You go, girl!" And then realize that you are only talking to the toddler on the training potty.
9. You chase escaped white mice from your daughter's science fair project around the baseboard of the living room on your hands and knees.
10. You bow to the dishwasher, offer burnt sacrifices on the altar of the range, and petition your refrigerator for frozen favors.
11. You hug your kids though the births... and life... and deaths... of guppies.

12. You convince your husband that painting the walls makes the couch look tacky, and that the new couch points out the faded carpet, and...

13. You choose your car's interior because it matches your outfit.

14. You can't decide if you are *Garfield's owner, Dennis's mother*, or *Blondie* when you decidedly don't feel comic.

15. Your shoulder pads take on a life of their own, and you have to beat them into submission.

16. You blame everything on El Nino (toilet run over? El Nino. Car won't start? El Nino. Pot burns? El Nino.)

17. You begin to call broccoli "little trees" and make airplane noises as you bring the spoon in for a landing.

18. You've got so much to do that you MUST start your day with prayer.

19. You and the cat stretch in tandem when the alarm rings.

20. You know that Henry David Thoreau was RIGHT!

21. You convince your chatty child that God only installed so many words on the human model, so if she uses them all up now, then she can't talk when she grows up.

22. You nick your shin during a nervous shave before the big job interview and the only band aid left in the house is green and printed with GI Joe.

23. Your marriage is a comfy pair of old blue jeans: stretched out in all the right places, still hugging

tightly where it counts, a little faded but ready for more wear, and having the rips all patched.

24. You enjoy old wood in the fire, old books in the hand, old friends in the heart.
25. You are crescendo when your job is decrescendo; you are in-tune when your family is off-key; you are harmony when the whole world is discord.
26. You faithfully use your treadmill each day.... on which to hang your laundry.
27. You rise through the layers of sleep, hear the pounding rain, feel the warmth of the quilt, see the wee hour, and sink again...
28. You keep three sizes of shoes in your closet, depending on which day of the month your feet decide to do the walking.
29. You decide that women's lib means never having to carry diapers in your purse again.
30. You peer into the heirloom mirror, and wonder if maybe, just maybe, your pioneer grandmother saw the same reflection.
31. Your body thinks a famine is coming and is storing up against the emergency.
32. You strain your spaghetti through a tennis racket.
33. Your "can do" attitude is a can of tuna, a can of peas, a can of French fried onions, and a can of cream of mushroom soup.
34. Your gallstone and college kid both pass in the same year.
35. You wear so many hats that you feel like a "nervous rack".

36. You can't catch your elderly parents at home and wonder what in the world they are up to.
37. You arrange the nursing home room for Grandma, the hospital room for Mom, the dorm room for daughter, and then wonder where there is room for . you.
38. You know that God loves you…. No matter what.

===

 And let us not grow weary of doing good, for in due season we will reap, if we do not give up.
Galatians 6:9

In all your ways acknowledge Him, and He will make straight your paths.
Proverbs 3:6

Meanderings: The day by day routine can become weary. Dealing with the same people, the same problems, the same outcomes can lead to frustration. What are some of the common daily frustrations that you encounter? How can acknowledging God make your path more straight? Do you know that God loves you, no matter what?

Father, Thank You for guiding me through the really big problems of life. But I sometimes forget to ask for Your guidance through the smaller, everyday situations. I find myself thinking that I am strong enough to handle it. I think that I should not bother You with my small problems. Forgive me for trying to take Your place. Forgive me for not coming to You with all my cares. And help to enjoy the common life!

To God be the glory

69. Ahhhh…. Chilled Air

When I was very young and living in a house that had no electricity, air conditioning was a paper fan on lollipop-looking stick from the funeral home. We would fan ourselves furiously, and when that failed, we would pump water over our heads, and run around, feeling the air cool our wet bodies. We had an ice box, not a refrigerator. It was literally a box with huge blocks of ice inside, and we would open it and lean against the ice. That was our normal; we had no thoughts that it would be different.

After my family hooked up to the REA lines that were being strung about the county, we had electricity and could run a rotating fan and a box fan. Moving air! And if it still got hot, we would wet a washcloth, drape it over the fan and sit in front of its refreshing coolness.

Electricity allowed us to exercise ingenious ideas to stay cool. Like the ice-box, the refrigerator open door poured out coolness… until our mother would yell at us for wasting electricity. We could freeze water into cubes of ice to suck on, rub on our bodies, or throw at each other.

We had heard of homes having air conditioning, where boxes were set in windows and poured out chilled air, but it seemed too fantastic to be true. However, one day, my aunt took me to the movies, and it was like walking into heaven to feel the chilled air float around my body, and all my sweat magically disappeared.

Not all businesses had air conditioning, but we found the few that did, and would spend time slowly walking their aisles, meticulously examining each tiny piece of merchandise, stretching the moment.

Poor farmers didn't have air conditioning, though, and later in my life, neither did poor college students. Then, I found that the houses that poor teachers could afford didn't have air conditioning, either. And this starts the story.

My husband and I designed and built a solar home with a minuscule budget. We learned our carpentry skills and allotted our money to include what we absolutely must have: plumbing, walls, floors, roof...but air conditioning remained as unaffordable and unreachable as our nonexistent drywall. We made do with our shell of a house because our dream and vision saw what it might be some day.

Over the years, walls slowly evolved, floors were carpeted, light fixtures were installed. We worked on a strict budget of both time and money. We still had no air conditioning; it was not a priority. Our lifestyle had never included it as a day by day necessity.

As we grew older, more affluent, more comfortable, values shifted. We did not have a radical change of philosophy, but we had a moderate change of mind. Air conditioning was a financial possibility at last. Did we want it? Did we need it? Would we be wiser to invest elsewhere? The hot dry summer of 1989 answered our questions.

We made all the arrangements with the air conditioning people, who came out with measuring tapes and notebooks, and mysterious conversion tables, and then gave us a date when they would start. It would be difficult, they said, to install air conditioning where none had existed before. It would be expensive, they warned, as this solar home had never needed a furnace. Nevertheless, we asked them to start before reason set in.

That's the basic plot. Now for the complications. Because of the drought of that hot summer, the yard surrounding our house began to develop some serious cracks, some deep enough that I could insert my foot. As the earth began to shift and compact, the foundation of the house began to settle and then to crack.

The crack in the basement wall demanded immediate attention, so we called the concrete people to check it out. They came out with measuring tapes, and notebooks, and mysterious conversion tables, and then gave us a date when they would start. It would be difficult, they said, as the entire back basement wall would have to be removed and replaced. It would be expensive, they warned, for labor and materials. Once again, we tossed reason. It had to be done.

Unfortunately, the two dates for air conditioning and concrete work coincided. We were assured that the two crews would not be in each other's way. And it was also the date in July when Grandma decided to take the bus down to visit with us. The three ring circus that developed would have made Barnum proud.

Each day, men in grimy overalls with insulated lunch boxes would park their pick ups anywhere in our yard, pull out boom boxes and assorted tools, and commence to assault our home: our lovingly crafted refuge of peace. No more peace. The concrete workers fired up their backhoe to dig a trench the depth of the basement, and used whining concrete saws to cut slits through the concrete. The dust was so choking and pervasive that anyone around had to wear a wet mask to trap the swirling dust and prevent it from getting into the lungs. We stuffed wet paper towels around all cracks in doorways and baseboards to prevent at least some of the dust from filtering into the house.

Meanwhile, the air conditioning men were trying to figure out how to put ductwork into a three story house where none had ever existed. They were crawling up ladders, dragging silvery tubes behind them, and then brazenly coming into my neat, freshly cleaned house and cutting holes through floors, carpet and all, and through walls where I had hung the perfect pictures.

Sometimes when the concrete men were prowling about the basement, the air-conditioning men would shout at them *WATCH OUT BELOW* as a chunk of wood suddenly fell. The concrete men would shout *WATCH OUT* when a block of cement slammed to the ground. Grandma shouted *WATCH OUT* whenever anything made a noise.

The concrete wall was not falling as nicely as the concrete men had hoped. They began wrapping chains through the slits, anchoring them to the backhoe and pulling. The entire basement wall shuddered and rippled like a flimsy paper towel caught in the wind. Grandma shuddered.

A series of two by fours was all that our entire house rested on at that moment. I feared that a deer (we lived next to a state park and wildlife was common) would barge into our cavernous basement, become terrified and knock the two by fours over. It did not happen; the props held, even through the relentless pulling of the chains.

Finally with one last groan, the wall gave up the struggle and crashed into the trench. The concrete men cheered. The air conditioning men cheered. Grandma cheered.

We passed around the Mountain Dew, wiped sweat and dust from our faces, and began to rebuild. As the new wall went up, the new furnace went in, metallic layer by layer. The silvery tubes were hammered and anchored into place; electric wires appeared from nowhere, and sharp shards of debris littered the basement floor. The air conditioning men sweat.

Outside, forms were placed for the concrete. Lumbering cement trucks rolled and heaved their contents, and the concrete men sweat. The temperature held steady at over 100 degrees; one worker passed out, and the electricity browned out. I worried about Grandma and pushed cold drinks to her.

Two days later, the heat intensified, rising another two or three degrees. The air grew suddenly still and in the west, we watched the thunderheads grow and billow, as the air turned green.

The concrete men were frantically completing the last details of their job before the storm broke, using the backhoe to fill in the trench, smoothing the overfills, wrapping fresh concrete in plastic and loading forms onto the trucks.

Inside, the air conditioning men were stringing the last few wires, trying to finish before the electrical storm struck. They set the thermostat, covered lines with black rubber, and began sweeping the floor of all traces of their work. The tension was palpable, with bickering and sniping between the workers.

As the air became more oppressive, the birds ceased singing. The frogs and crickets became still. It began to get darker and greener. Whippoorwills, thinking it was dusk, began to call, and then, almost embarrassedly, they stopped. The wind picked up, ruffling the concrete workers' hair, then swooping up odd pieces of paper and leaves, and finally swirling small dust funnels. The concrete men gave a final check to their work, asked us to inspect, and left.

The air conditioning men were ready to try the thermostat. A bright flash of light startled all of us, as did the sharp crash of thunder. One air conditioning man hesitated, bit his lip, and then continued to set it. Just as the first patter of ran hit the roof, the air conditioner kicked on. We each ran to a different register and stood over it, greedily reveling in the chilled air pouring over our chests and faces. Grandma cried in relief; I joined her.

I remember when, as a child, we first got running water in our house, and we put in a bathroom. All of us kids wanted to be the first to flush, so we drew straws for that privilege. And for several days after, we would sometimes flush for the heck of it, just to marvel at the new invention. But later, we took it for granted and thought no more of it. So it was with the air conditioner.

I turned it on today and it began to pour out chilled air. I thought back again to the funeral home fans and box fans and rotating fans, of open Frigidaire doors, and the busy lazy hours in department stores, soaking in the chilled air. I recalled that hectic summer, the gray gritty dust, flaring tempers, sweat rolling in rivulets down my back, crushed Mountain Dew cans trickling golden nectar that attracted wasps, and the broken tools and empty bank account. Then I turned away, taking it for granted, one more part of life that was ordinary.

==

But seek first His kingdom and His righteousness, and all these things will be added to you.
Matthew 6:33

For which of you, desiring to build a tower, does not first sit down and count the cost, whether he has enough to complete it?
Luke 14:28

Meanderings: Choices. Priorities. Sometimes it is difficult to make the right choices, and choose the right priorities. It's not that I don't want the right choices; it's just difficult. Putting in air conditioning was a choice. After much consideration of financial priorities, after consulting with experts, after praying, we came to the conclusion that this was the right move. Have you had to make choices, or choose priorities that caused you to pray, to seek God's will, to consider carefully your life and situation?

Father, some parts of life are not easy. Thank You for Your guidance through this process. We thank You for the marvelous invention of air conditioning! Help me to remember to seek You and Your will as I continue to make decisions. Help bring Scripture to mind when I need Your Word.

To God be the glory

70. Thoughts of a 12 Year Old Runner

I am running the 300 yard dash.

I'm at the starting line and the starter said, "Are you ready? Get set... *GO!*" We are off. My eyes are closed because I am concentrating on my running, on my feet slapping the ground.

Then comes the turn. I am rounding it when I hear the pounding of feet and feel breath on my neck. Then I take off faster and it all fades away.

Now the last stretch. I am sweating hard and it runs into my eyes. It starts to burn, so I close my eyes again and blink. I close on another guy and start to run harder and harder. We are neck and neck.

I pass him, and again feel breath on my neck and hear the pounding feet. It fades again. At the finish line, I try so hard, so hard, and cross it. But I am second. And I am proud.

(Written by Luke Parson)

==

Therefore, since we are surrounded by such a great cloud of witnesses, let us throw off everything that hinders and the sin that so easily entangles. And let us run with perseverance the race marked out for us.
Hebrews 12:1

I have fought the good fight, I have finished the race, I have kept the faith.
2 Tim. 4: 7

You were running a good race. Who cut in on you to keep you from obeying the truth?
Galatians 5: 7

Do you not know that in a race all the runners run, but only one gets the prize? Run in such a way as to get the prize.
Everyone who competes in the games goes into strict training. They do it to get a crown that will not last, but we do it to get a crown that will last forever.
Therefore I do not run like someone running aimlessly; I do not fight like a boxer beating the air.
No, I strike a blow to my body and make it my slave so that after I have preached to others, I myself will not be disqualified for the prize.
1 Corinthians 9: 24-27

Meanderings: To train, to run... to focus on the path... to not look back... to pace yourself... to cross the finish line: this is the essence of running the race. How is our life like a race? What can disrupt the race, causing you to either not finish or finish poorly? How do these Scriptures influence you when running the race?

Father, I want to finish this life race well. I want to receive Your prize of eternal life. I want to make a difference to all those who are running with me. Help me to not get distracted. Help me discard all that might hinder me. Thank You for the encouraging Scriptures that urge me to run with perseverance.

To God be the glory

71. The Cards

Just before Christmas, I had to buy a new box of sympathy cards. Still another co-worker's parent had died, and when I reached into the box under the desk, it was empty.

That particular box, gold foil covered, was a relic of the 1940s and had belonged to my grandmother. Grandma was a great one for sending cards. The little bookcase by her phone was stacked to overflowing with boxes of cards: birthday, sympathy, anniversary and marriage, get well, thinking of you, and blank notes. Some were boxes that she had purchased, some had been gifts from folks who knew that Grandma liked to send cards, and several were from charitable organizations such as Veterans of Foreign Wars. Those cards all had little pictures of Betsy Ross and flags, and said "Support your veterans" on the back.

When Grandma died, Grandpa valiantly kept up the card tradition. Cards for our holy days, our man-made days, and our special celebrations kept coming from Grandma's stash. Then Grandpa grew feeble and had to move to a nursing home.

The farm auction was sad. Grandpa sat in the middle of the auction looking at others pawing through all his memories. The boxes of cards had been placed into one huge box to be sold as a group. Grandpa looked especially sad as he saw the haphazard tumble of card boxes. He touched them reverently.

"Your grandma," he told me, "always sent cards. Didn't matter if she barely knew the folks. Us living way out here in the country and all, she didn't get out much. But she sure did send those cards."

I picked up the box and gave Grandpa five dollars. It probably would not have brought any more than that on the block, and that way he had no commission to pay. The cards went home with me and I continued Grandma and Grandpa's tradition.

Sending cards had never been a big deal with me. The telephone was so handy; I could just reach out and touch. But I made a commitment to use the cards.

Some were yellowed and the glue no longer worked on the envelopes. Some had little spongy tabs pasted to them with bits of gilded paper that popped out when the card was opened. Some had inlays of lace. It was easy to see the styles of the decades on the cards: the bright oranges of the 70s, the silver and turquoise of the 50s, the innocent playful animals of the 40s. Slowly, slowly the collection of cards dwindled as I remembered the special days of family, friends, neighbors, and co-workers.

One card that I sent a co-worker was especially yellowed. His father had died after a lingering illness. When I gave Tim the card, I also enclosed a little note about Grandma's tradition, and that this was the last of her cards. Tim told me later that the note meant so much, and that it helped him feel connected a little longer to his father's memory.

The deaths continued. I remember Grandpa saying that he was so old that no one was left who remembered the things that he remembered. They had all died. It seemed as if people were dying all around me, also. And so, with shock, I reached into the gold box, and found it empty.

A co-worker's son had died of leukemia. Our friend Dave's mother had died from cancer on Friday, and my neighbor's father had died of pneumonia on Saturday. I purchased a new box of cards. "10 Sympathy Cards With Envelopes" the box said. I opened a few cards.

"Words cannot truly express the deep sorrow that is felt by so many people."
"Thoughts are with you today and always."
"Wishing you peace and comfort."

They just weren't the same. And yet, the tradition
continued. I added a personal note to Dave and to Mary
and to Marti, and sent the envelopes on their way.

Grandma, I wish I could send you a card, too. A thank
you card. You and Grandpa were apples of gold in
settings of silver (see Proverbs 25:11)
===

 *Finally, all of you, be like-minded, be
sympathetic, love one another, be
compassionate and humble.*
1 Peter 3:8

*Therefore, as God's chosen people, holy and dearly
loved, clothe yourselves with compassion, kindness,
humility, gentleness and patience.*
Colossians 3:12

*Rejoice with those who rejoice; mourn with those who
mourn.*
Romans 12:15

*If anyone has material possessions and sees a brother or
sister in need but has no pity on them, how can the love
of God be in that person?*
1 John 3:17

Meanderings: Lives are saved and enriched with compassion. Just the right word... at the right time.... can make a lasting difference to another person. How can you be an encourager? How can you show compassion to one in sorrow or grief? How can you rejoice with others?

Father, help me speak fitly spoken words, words that can console and encourage. If I can't find the words, help me to know how to show compassion. I want to be that friend indeed to one in need, but sometimes I need Your nudge and guidance. Thank you for the many times others have shown love to me when I needed it most.

To God be the glory

72. Pigs Do What Pigs Do

I absentmindedly scratched the head of my calf. It was a warm spring day with a nice breeze, and I sat by my calf in the lush grass. She hadn't been mine for very long, and I wanted to have a bond with her. I had dreams of owning her for several years, and even more dreams were connected with her.

As I groomed her with a curry comb, she seemed to enjoy the light scratching along her back. Her rough tongue ran along my hand as I rubbed her nose. And her big brown eyes looked into mine, and then back to the grass before her.

It was the early 1960s. I was finishing eighth grade and looking forward to high school. My friends had all begun to talk about clubs and band and cheer and boyfriends and college. Out of all of those topics, I could only talk about band. I had no interest in cheerleading. Probably I would try to join a club. And boyfriends and college? Distant dreams. Very distant.

I was at the age where I began to realize my strengths and talents. And I was all too aware of my deficits. I was skinny and short, with crooked teeth and a too-long nose. Not exactly boyfriend material. Painfully shy, I could not even imagine a boy looking into my eyes the way my calf did. And would I fit into some club? The only thing I could do halfway well was write. But there was no writing club.

And about college. I wanted to go to college. It seemed like a great goal. But was I smart enough? And what did I want to become? And I had no money. Scholarships? Would I ever qualify? The future seemed foggy.

We lived on a farm several miles from town. While my town friends were looking forward to getting jobs babysitting and working at the soda fountain, I was stuck on the farm with no means of transportation. So a job in town was out of the question. How was I ever to get money together to go to college?

Those years were rough for farmers. My dad not only farmed but also took a job in town on the 3 to 11 shift. That way he could farm from sunrise until about 2:00, go to his job in town, get home between 11:00 and midnight, and be back up early to continue farming. I knew better than to ask my parents to fund my college plans.

But Mom and Dad had a plan. They gave me a calf. The deal was that I would care for the calf, and they would furnish the pasture. If there were vet bills, they would pay with the expectation that I would pay them back as money came in from the calf. The goal was that this calf would have a calf. If it was a heifer, then both would have calves, and so on. The money from selling those calves could pay for college, along with any scholarships that I might be able to earn.

I was delighted. The calf became my 4-H project as well as the path to my education. And so, I spent time just laying against my calf while she rested in the pasture. I combed her, washed her, untangled her tail.

The time came when she was old enough to become pregnant. When we learned that she was carrying a calf, my delight knew no end. As she progressed, my dad suggested that I take her out of the pasture and put her in the barn lot so that I could keep a closer eye on her. Dad said that first births for a cow could be difficult.

Everything seemed to go well. Everything, that is, until the Sunday night when we all went to church. My calf was quite swollen and was pacing. But Dad said she had not gone into labor yet and showed no signs, so he felt that it was safe for us to attend church for an hour. As soon as we returned home, I rushed out to the barnyard to check on her.

What I found was horrifying. While we were at church, the pigs had broken a fence and were out in the lot. At the same time, my calf had gone into labor and was helpless on the ground. Pigs are carnivores and vicious. They had attacked my calf while she was down, and had eaten though her belly and eaten the unborn calf. My calf was moaning and bellowing and her beautiful liquid brown eyes were rolling back and forth. I screamed, grabbed a two by four board and began hitting at the pigs in my rage.

Dad heard the commotion and came running. He took in the situation in one glance, and told me to go the porch and get his rifle.

"Yes!" I cried. "Yes! Kill everyone of those pigs!"

Dad took a deep breath. "No, Diana," he replied. "Pigs do what pigs do. But your calf is not going to make it. We need to put her out of her misery."

So unfair. So unfair. I kept muttering while I trekked to the house to get the rifle. So terribly unfair. When I gave my dad the gun, he gave me a choice. I could stay and watch or return to the house.

As I turned and walked back, I heard the sharp *CRACK* and knew that my calf was dead. My dreams were dead. My heart felt dead.

Would my parents give me another calf? The short answer was no. They told me that I could buy one of their calves, paying for it as money came in. It was a hard fact of life: While there are some breaks, not everything is given free.

A few weeks later in that tumultuous year, my grandfather died of cancer. He was such a loving and gentle man, who treated me like a princess. He was the type of grandpa who bought me a jar of olives because he knew that I liked olives and knew that my parents did not have the money for such a luxury. He was the type of grandpa who pulled out the chair for me at the table. He was the grandpa who took me fishing.

How terribly unfair for cancer to strike him. So unfair. I knew there were bad men in the world who didn't get cancer, so why my grandpa? Totally unjust.

As I fought back tears, I remembered my dad's words: Pigs do what pigs do. And in Grandpa's case, cancer does what cancer does. I could spend the rest of my life in burning anger at pigs and cancer. Or I could acknowledge that some things were not in my control.

"My ways are not your ways," said God.

God had quite dramatically shown me that I was not in control, but that His plans were greater than mine. I did buy another calf on a time-pay basis. That calf lived through birthing, and I built a very small herd. I sold them, and with the scholarships and grants and work-study jobs that I earned, college became a reality. And I missed my grandpa so much, but time worked a healing in my heart, and I replaced my rage with memories.

Even today when things like tornados and floods and accidents and covid happen, I have to take a deep breath and tell myself that pigs do what pigs do. And thanks to the trauma of "then" and to the gentle grace of God, I can handle the "now" much better. His ways certainly were not my ways. I would not have chosen this method to obtain this wisdom and meet my dreams. But I choose to believe God and these were His ways.

(Dedicated to my parents: Kenneth and Violet Mae Newquist)

(Chosen for future publication in *Mountains, Molehills and the Good Stuff Between*, compiled by Rita Klundt)

==

Teach me to do Your will,
For You are my God;
Let Your good Spirit lead me on level ground.
Psalm 143: 10

Then the Lord your God will prosper you abundantly in all the work of your hand, in the offspring of your body and in the offspring of your cattle and in the produce of your ground, for the Lord will again rejoice over you for good, just as He rejoiced over your fathers.
Deuteronomy 30:9

Give thanks in all circumstances; for this is the will of God in Christ Jesus for you.
1 Thessalonians 5: 18

Meanderings: I was absolutely crushed at such a young age by the deaths of my calf and my grandfather. But God led me through it, and I learned valuable life lessons. Have you had a crushing experience that God used to teach you His will? To equip you for the future? Did you accept His will, or beat against it?

Father, hard as it may be, I do thank You for the difficult parts of life. Without those valleys, I would not recognize the mountains. I would not be equipped for climbing them. I pray now for those who are looking in the face of the impossible, wondering what hardship will come next. I pray for their perseverance and strength in You.

To God be the glory

73. You Were My Students

I owe you so much.

I began teaching in 1971. And now I'm retired.
Facebook has a way of reminding me of how much I
loved teaching and loved my students (well, most of
them.... lol!). How gratifying to see former students now
being wonderful grandparents and wise parents. I love
reading of your interactions with your children and
grandchildren.

Some of my students went into education, some teaching
in public, some in private schools, and some
homeschooling. I so hope that I and your other teachers
gave you positive inspiration to go this route, and I hope
that you find the uncommon joy that I did in teaching.

But my students have also gone into so many other
directions, and I am proud to read of your efforts and
accomplishments, yes, even of your disappointments.
You don't have disappointments unless you have strived.

I'm glad to read of your travels, knowing how travel is an
education in itself. I'm glad to read your wit and your
musings. Whether you were one of my students from my
last semester or from 1971, know that I find you to be
fascinating people.

I've had down times in my career: the student who is behind bars now. The students who died, whether from disease, war, accident, or self destruction. I wish I could have saved you from that. I'm sad to learn of students who have families disintegrate or have job loss. Although some students have come to faith, others have lost faith. I'd like to turn back the pages to when we wrote or spoke about such things and they were only hypothetical. School is a reality of its own, and life outside of school carries another sense of reality. I wish that I had used literature and composition and speech and drama and journalism in a better way to help you with that transition of realities.

My students have made me laugh. So many times I came home and doubled over with laughter relating to Hubby what someone said or wrote, or how someone played a scene. I'll never forget the young man who excitedly told me that his sister was late having her first baby, and that the doctor was going to have to "seduce" her. Please know I never laughed AT you. You may have unwittingly caused the mirth, but I never found YOU to be the one to be made fun of.

My students have made me cry. Some of the writings and speeches were so poignant, so laced with honest emotion, that I teared up. The student who came in to tell me that her parents were divorcing and that she didn't know who to live with. The student who tearfully told me she was quitting school; she was pregnant; she didn't know what to do. The student whose mother died while he was at school one morning. You have met and carried the hard parts of life. I wish I could have erased those times for you.

My students have made me think and sometimes change my position. I'll never forget the young lady who courageously gave a very graphic speech on abortion. She cemented in my mind that this was an absolute wrong. My debate students dived into research and challenged my thinking deeply.

My students have written and spoken in ways that I admire. One young man became a Missouri senator and is eloquent speaking about life. My students who wrote poetry found such unique and wonderful ways to express life (I wish I could have signed my name to some of those writings). And some of their poetry was done just laying on the floor with a pile of words in front of them, and then thinking about how to arrange them. Awesome!

I admire my journalism students, who were honor students and still put in the crazy long hours to put out a newspaper and yearbook. They went after the story and the story behind the story, and the angle, and the personality. They developed leadership that was unbelievable. I really think I could have died in a corner of the classroom and they would just keep on leading and teaching themselves.

I admire my speech and drama students and how they made their characters and speeches some to life. Such long hours of practice and weekends of contest and productions. Bravo! Bravo! In a way, it was a safe method of trying on life.

Literature and composition students continually spoke up or wrote about characters that gave me insight in a different way. Such joy to me to see you connecting all the dots between an author and his times and history and your own present time and your own situations.

Although I always wanted you to excel in the classroom, it was more important to me to see you become good people, good citizens, good parents, good employees. I was more interested in having you be honest than be a straight A student. I valued your integrity more than your grade point average. I wanted you to be creative and to explore, even when it went outside the curriculum box. I wanted you to learn how to learn, for no one can ever take that away from you.

If you were my student during the past 40 years, know that I am still cheering you on. Don't ever give up!! You are too important! Thanks for putting up with me; you taught me so much.

(Dedicated to all my former students)

==

I will instruct you and teach you in the way
you should go;
I will counsel you with My loving eye on you.
Psalm 32:8

The fear of the Lord is the beginning of knowledge,
but fools despise wisdom and instruction.
Proverbs 1:7

Teach me Your way, Lord,
that I may rely on Your faithfulness;
give me an undivided heart,
that I may fear Your name.
Psalm 86:11

Let My teaching fall like rain
and My words descend like dew,
like showers on new grass,
like abundant rain on tender plants.
Deuteronomy 32:2

Meanderings: I give praise for the legacy of teaching... As I was taught by my teachers, I also taught my students. Who is a teacher who impacted your life? What would you like to say to the many teachers in your life? How is God your greatest teacher?

Father, please never stop teaching me. I need Your gentle lessons in how to conduct my life, how to treat others, and how to understand Your Word. Thank You for the uncommon joy I found in education, and for the many students and co-workers You put on my path. I ask You to bless them.... And draw them to Yourself. Open their eyes, Father, to Who You are.

To God be the glory

74. Hot Buttered Dr. Pepper

"Mind your manners. Clean your plate. Thank you 'mam." Those were but a few of the maxims that my parents taught us about the grace and art of living. Holiday excitement was to be no excuse for a lapse of politeness. And, whatever we learned of etiquette was to be multiplied four-fold when we visited Grandma.

Something about Grandma: her dignity, her carriage and posture, her warm and selfless manner. She both inspired and awed us. Even if my parens had not drilled us in the Post and Vanderbilt tradition, we still would have stood to attention for Grandma.

One memorable Christmas Eve, Grandma invited us to supper. We children were reminded of the basics on the drive to her house. Don't raid the trash (Grandma got the most interesting junk mail), don't tell Grandma that you don't like the food, and don't ask to leave the table before everyone is done eating, even if you have to go to the bathroom BAD.

Grandma did things right. She seated us in the living room, as though we were visiting royalty in her mansion, and served us a before dinner dink, non-alcoholic, of course. She had found a new recipe for hot buttered Dr. Pepper. Unfortunately, everyone in my family considered the beverage to be only slightly less repulsive than back-alley cough syrup. Grandma entered with a tray of crystal cups filled with the steaming liquid. We each dutifully took a cup, murmured "thank you" and rolled our eyes to the ceiling when Grandma left the room. My mother choked hers down, but the rest of us ungrateful urchins were gagged by the smell.

"Mom, please drink mine," begged one little sister in a whisper. "I just can't."

"Pass it down, then," my mother whispered back.

Thus began the famous cup brigade, remembered to this day by everyone except Grandma. In no time at all, the entire family was busily passing cups around the circle to my mother, who then passed on the empties.

Grandma bustled back just as Mom was downing the sixth and last cup.

"Oh, I'm so glad that you liked it," Grandma beamed. "Here's more." And she proceeded to refill all of our cups. None of us dared protest. As soon as Grandma returned to the kitchen to check the ham, the brigade began again. My mother looked about desperately for a thirsty potted plant, but alas. Cups seven through 12 went down more slowly, but Mom quaffed the last one and set her cup down in relief.

Relief did not last long. Grandma, amazed by the success of her new recipe, poured the third and last round before dinner, and Mom set the world's record of drinking 18 cups of hot buttered Dr. Pepper in one night. She hit the bathroom before we sat down to eat, but as the evening went on, we could tell that she was seriously reconsidering the rule about not leaving the table before everyone was done eating. If we so much as looked longingly at another roll, Mom gave us the evil eye. And when Grandma asked if we wanted to take a break and open gifts before dessert, the loudest YES came from my mother.

Funny. The need for politeness lectures was gone. Why my mother did that for us is still a mystery, but she set a better example than any lecture could.

==

 And as you wish that others would do to you, do so to them.
Luke 6:31

Be not deceived: evil communications corrupt good manners.
1 Corinthians 15: 33
Let your speech always be gracious, seasoned with salt, so that you may know how you ought to answer each person.
Colossians 4:6

Meanderings: What manners and politeness lessons were you taught? How can good manners make situations better? Do you see manners changing within your lifetime? How does the use of politeness advance the Kingdom?

Father, let my actions, and words and manners always speak well of You. Do not let me lead someone astray because of my language or actions. Let me treat each person with whom I come into contact as I would want to be treated. Thank You for the grace in my life, and help me treat others with similar grace.

To God be the glory

75. Bill's Chair

The old battered lawn chair was the first thing I noticed in my neighbor's yard when we moved into the neighborhood. We bought the blue foursquare on the corner, next to a green Tudor-style half timber. The houses on the block faced a park. It wasn't a park with playground equipment or ball fields or picnic tables. Just a large, nice green area, with some walking trails and a few benches. People walked their dogs, held hands and strolled, and some ran. The chair in my neighbor's yard was a perfect viewing spot of the park activity.

I soon learned that the chair actually was for another purpose. I walked out to my front yard one afternoon soon after settling into the home, and met Bill. The chair was Bill's chair. It was a somewhat black, somewhat green metal lawn chair of a style popular probably in the '20s. Other than the less than impressive color and a multitude of dings, the chair was in good shape: sturdy and balanced. And it had a strand of clear Christmas tree lights strung across the back rim. Bill was sitting in his chair, watching the walkers in the park, and puffing on a cigar.

He looked at me as I drew closer.

"Want a cigar? I'm Bill."

"No, thanks. And I"m Joe."

"Pull up a chair, Joe."

And so I did. Somewhere in our garage was a metal folding chair. I unfolded it and set it next to Bill. Bill's chair was in a tight corner of land bordered by the sidewalk and the low wrought iron fence that separated our properties. I set my chair cautiously on my side of the fence and close to the sidewalk. Bill's chair had rounded legs, but mine had four separate legs that immediately began to sink into the damp soil.

Bill came out to his chair every day at about the same time to smoke his cigar. He mentioned that his wife didn't allow him to smoke in the house. And besides, he liked watching the activity in the park. When someone came by on the sidewalk, Bill talked to them.

Sometimes a passing car would honk. Bill would wave. I grew to enjoy my afternoons with Bill, despite his cigar.

Sometimes we talked. Sometimes we just nodded and watched the park and the traffic. Bill was disgusted with the government, and pot holes. He was worried about the big maple in the park that might be dying. He liked dogs, but not the ones who wandered around without an owner. He enjoyed ice cream almost as much as his cigar, and sometimes his wife came out with a bowl full for each of us.

All in all, it was pleasant. My wife met Bill''s wife. We learned that we all had kids in a distant state. We all enjoyed retirement. My wife would sometimes bring out a brownie or bottles of water.

The weather made no difference to Bill. This is a state with four seasons, and Bill was in his chair even if snow was falling, or it was raining, or sultry. In particularly bad storms, he smoked more quickly, and he also had a rain slicker for downpours. In those situations, I yelled out the garage at Bill, but didn't go out, myself. I sometimes expected him to be struck by lightning and just explode right there in his chair.

I asked Bill about the Christmas lights on the chair. He couldn't remember when he first put them on, but it was whenever the battery strands first came out. He had gone through several strands, and thought that it added a bit of class to the chair. I couldn't disagree. He left the lights on 24/7 and it had become the neighborhood night light.

Time passed in that leisurely haze of neighborly friendship, but Bill and his wife never invited us into their home. We had asked them to come over for pizza, but they were busy. The next time there was another excuse. So we continued to have that front yard relationship and really… that was not bad.

After several years, Bill's wife died. We went to pay our respects. Bill was sitting at the funeral home by the coffin, silently crying. I shook his hand; my wife gave him a hug. He thanked us for coming, and then just stared blankly at the wall. We met his children, a son and daughter. That afternoon, after the funeral, Bill was once again out in his chair, and the children had gone back home.

I was surprised that he wasn't smoking his cigar in the house, now that his wife was gone. Bill mentioned that, saying that he just wanted to keep on respecting her. And so each afternoon, Bill continued to smoke one cigar in his front yard chair. We continued to talk about high taxes, and whether the Cubs had a chance this year, and what kind of fertilizer to use on the grass.

My wife discreetly would bring out sandwiches, and have some extra for Bill to take home. Then she would add some cookies, and sometimes a carton of milk. Bill never turned it down.

One afternoon, Bill did not come out. I waited for him, but after a while, I knocked on his door. He finally answered, wearing some stained pajamas and a robe. He looked awful. I asked him if he needed to see the doctor, but he waved that idea away. Between wheezing and coughing, he could barely talk, and had to sit down. I told him that we were going to get him some help. He didn't turn it down, and we called 911.

The ambulance came and took Bill to the hospital. We visited him there every day, but pneumonia was claiming him. I wondered how to get a hold of his children. I asked the nurse if Bill had a wallet with him, and if she could look in it to see if there were any phone numbers or mention of his kids. She found a number, and I contacted the son.

Both children were there the next day, and were by Bill's side when he died. They shook my hand and thanked me for caring for Bill and being his friend. They mentioned that at a later time, they would be back to clean out the house.

A couple of weeks later, a large green dumpster was on the front yard. I was amazed at how much was tossed into it. I talked to the son, asked if I could help in anyway, and he smiled.

"Mom and Dad kept everything," he told me. "It got worse as they grew older, so now we have lots to get rid of. We checked with Good Will and a couple of churches, but no one really wanted what they had. Seems a shame, but…."

I watched as a perfectly good piano was carefully rolled into the dumpster. The daughter watched it with tears, and then said to me, "We couldn't even give it away. Hoping that the dump treats it kindly."

I understood. It was a time of life that almost everyone goes through. Sorting through the "stuff"... Making decisions ... Realizing that what is precious to you is precious to no one else ... Understanding that memories live on, and perhaps that is the best way to handle the "stuff".

Bill and his wife never had "stuff" outside. Other neighbors had little picket fences around flower beds, flags, gnome statues, and the like. But Bill only had his chair outside, and hostas that didn't need much attention. Their "stuff" was inside: clothes, books, dishes, stacks of magazines. The kitchen appliances were from another decade. So were the clothes. No one bought books anymore. And so the dumpster filled.

One afternoon, the son came by to thank us again for being Bill's friend, and for watching after him. We shook hands, and I assured him that his father was a good man. The son said that the dumpster would be moved in a day or two, and then the house would be sold at auction.

The next day when I stepped outside to get the mail, I realized that the landscape was different. Bill's chair was gone. I went to the dumpster, but could not see inside, and I was too old to climb it and dumpster dive. So I dragged a ladder out of the garage and propped it up on the side of the dumpster.

The chair was lying sideways on top of some broken lamps and frayed towels, the Christmas lights still dangling. I tugged at the chair, but it was built like a WW2 tank and I just could not budge it. About that time a couple kids walked by, and I hollered at them.

"Hey! Can you help me get this chair out of the trash?"

The teens looked at each other and at me. First they helped me get down. Then one climbed the ladder and easily tossed the chair, as if it was made of styrofoam, down to his friend.

"Anything else, Mister?"

I thanked them, offered cookies which they declined, and dragged the chair to my side of the wrought iron fence. I tested the Christmas lights; they still worked. Then I settled down in the chair, sans cigar, and watched the people in the park.

Bill's chair. Good memories. Good "stuff."

===

For we brought nothing into the world, and we can take nothing out of it. But if we have food and clothing, we will be content with that.
1 Timothy 6:7-8

Do not store up for yourselves treasures on earth, where moths and vermin destroy, and where thieves break in and steal. But store up for yourselves treasures in heaven, where moths and vermin do not destroy, and where thieves do not break in and steal.
Matthew 6:19-20

So we fix our eyes not on what is seen, but on what is unseen, since what is seen is temporary, but what is unseen is eternal.
2 Corinthians 4:18

Meanderings: "Stuff." It seems to grow and take on a life of its own. What "stuff" are you hanging on to? Why is it so hard to let go? Are they your treasures on earth? Are you fixing your eyes on what is eternal?

Father, I am guilty. I keep too much "stuff." Help me to seek Your kingdom more than I seek treasure here on earth. Thank You for supplying all that I need. And help me decide on how to best use the excess for Your glory. Cleanse my heart and mind of the anxiety of too much "stuff."

To God be the glory

76. Until the Water Runs Out

She stretched her arm up, and tugged at the constrictive sleeve. We were the only two on the tour bus, as the others had gone to see the lighthouse overlooking the Mississippi River. There were too many steps for me to navigate with my cane, and the other lady, I learned, was recovering from breast cancer and just didn't have the stamina.

Her name was Beth. She said that her husband, Bently, wanted for the two of them to come on this trip to Hannibal. But he failed to think through all the situations where she just could not keep up. So she and I sat in the bus while the rest toured the cave and walked up the cliff to the lighthouse.

I didn't mind sitting out part of the tour, and Beth was a good companion. She told me about the breast cancer... How they had not given her much hope. How they had messed up the lymph so that she had to wear the compression sleeve and keep her arm up for drainage. She talked about Bently. They had been teachers, then fell in love. She regaled me with stories of their travels: of how Bently always got lost, but in doing so he found the most fascinating people and places. Their adventures took them around the world, with strange foods, weird housing, and wild transportation.

Sometimes a sudden friendship clicks… kindred spirits… separated at birth kind of friends. Our conversation never stopped, wandered into intimate confessions and tear-blinding laughter. It was almost jarring to have the group come back to the bus with their chatter and shared photos of the lighthouse and the river and all the flowers lining the steps.

Our next stop took us down to the historic district, where we had time to wander and explore the shops and the Twainish homes. Bently wanted to see the Twain museum and homes. Beth and I decided to visit the antique and curio shops.

We must have looked a sight: me with my cane and Beth with her arm held high. We passed a coffee shop and at the same instant decided to stop for coffee before exploring any further. The coffee shop was shabby chic, and we settled back into comfy old chairs and put our feet up on the little table in front of us. Our conversation continued as if we had never stopped for a short bus ride. I confided to Beth that taking this trip was difficult for me. I was recently widowed, had developed a hip pain that would probably lead to replacement surgery and had to use a cane. I was determined to not hide at home mourning, but there were times when I wondered if I was sane to make this trip all by myself.

For the first time, our conversation paused. Beth finally spoke again, but slowly. She told me how she had about six months to live, how Bently was not taking it well, how he wanted this one more trip together. She confessed that she was pushing Bently to explore on his own, without her, preparing him for the day when she would not be by his side every moment.

She paused again.

"I can't imagine not... being," she whispered. "I've lived in this skin for 55 years. I can't imagine not being here. I'm not afraid to die, but I fear for Bently not having me to help him to not get lost."

As we left the coffee shop, we both noticed at the same time the little woodpecker bobbing up and down into the glass of water.

"I used to watch this in science class," I told her. "I think it was something about evaporation."

Beth agreed. "Bently taught science. He had one of those birds in his classroom."

"Up and down, up and down," I said.

"Until he ran out of water... And just stopped." Beth continued.

We looked at each other.

"That's me," she said. "All this glamour." She waved her good arm around the coffee shop. "And then when the water runs out… The end."

We both began to cry and sank into the coffee shop couch. I held her as she sobbed. We fished out hankies, dabbed our eyes, and continued outside. We had more to see, more to say.

Three months later, the tour guide sent the group a short note from Bently. Beth had died. He thanked us for being new friends and helping them enjoy the trip. And at the end of the note was a sketch.

It was a woodpecker. Bobbing.

(Dedicated to Barbara Beller and Dee Shaul)

(Published in Ekphrastic Review, June 2021)

==

And I heard a voice from heaven saying, "Write this: Blessed are the dead who die in the Lord from now on." "Blessed indeed," says the Spirit, "that they may rest from their labors, for their deeds follow them!"
Revelation 14:13

Jesus said to him, "I am the way, and the truth, and the life. No one comes to the Father except through Me."
John 14:6

For God so loved the world, that He gave His only Son, that whoever believes in Him should not perish but have eternal life.
John 3: 16

Meanderings: We do not know Beth's spiritual state. She mentions not being afraid to die, but she mentions nothing about the Lord. Are you afraid to die? Do you have assurance that if you died right now, that you would be in Heaven? Do you believe the simplicity of John 3:16? It is too important to NOT make a decision for Jesus.

Father, I hold tightly to Your promise that if I believe Jesus is Who He said He is, then I am a follower of Christ and will have eternity in Heaven. I desire eternity with You. I totally believe that it is possible to know my destiny after death. Thank You for saving someone like me. I pray that You help me spread the good news of the way, the truth and the life.

To God be the glory

77. Two Man Sled

The first sled that my brother Lynn and I had was short with fading lettering and one broken board. Mom bought it for us at a yard sale. Lynn and I struggled all winter to have fun with that sled. But the sled was so short that we couldn't "belly- drive" it. Instead we had to squeeze up while sitting on our rears and steer with our feet.

We must have complained a lot about the short sled because next Christmas we were given a brand new, five-foot long sled. It had shiny varnish and a painted brand name that could still be read. And it was so long that I could lay down on my stomach and my feet would just barely hang over the end.

Lynn and I decided that we would try out both of the sleds that very afternoon. And instead of staying on some of the smaller hills on our farm, we pulled the sleds a couple of miles down the road to get to the Vincennes road hill, a steep hill with a wicked turn halfway down that curved sharply to the left.

Lynn and I took turns with each sled the rest of the afternoon. One of us would "belly-drive" the long sled while the other one would try to make it down the hill with "Shorty." That little sled would do fine until the curve. And then, no matter how much I would lean to the right, it would never make that turn. Having to sit up just raised the center of gravity too high. I just couldn't make the curve. But "Long-boy" was a different story. A running belly flop start sent me flashing down the hill. And dragging the right leg would pull me around the curve, flying down the road to the little town below. By the time Shorty had dumped Lynn and he had picked himself up, Long-boy was already at the bottom and I was beginning the walk back up.

As the sun was beginning to set, Lynn and I realized that we needed to head home soon. But we each wanted to take just one more ride. So we hit on an idea. We would use Long-boy as a two-man sled. And being the older and larger of the two, it was decided that I would lay down first. Then my bother took a running start and belly flopped onto my back. At first we started out slowly but then gathered speed. And struggling to hold on, Lynn grabbed on to me, pressing both my legs against the sled. I struggled to get my right leg loose, but I just couldn't get it free. And so we did not make the turn.

Instead we shot straight across the road and plowed into the shallow drainage ditch along the roadside. When we hit the frozen gravel piled along the edge of the road, Long-boy came to a sudden halt. But Lynn and I did not. In an instant I became the sled! We continued sliding onward for another ten feet or so until we plowed to a stop. I had snow inside my coat, under my shirt, and even behind my glasses, which had somehow stayed on my face. I pushed Lynn off me and tried to clean my glasses. We lay there laughing in the snow, enjoying the thrill of the ride, excitedly retelling to each other what had just happened.

As I sat up, I noticed that my heavy winter coat was open. At first I thought that it had been unzipped during the ride. But instead, the coat was cut completely through. And the shirt beneath was also slightly cut. Only the Long Johns underneath the shirt were untouched. Then we saw that we had slid through a trash pile that someone had dumped along the roadside. Digging through the snow, we found the jagged bottom of a broken mayonnaise jar. If the coat had been thinner, or my layering of clothing less, it would have been my stomach that had been slit open.

We walked slowly home, pulling the sleds. We were thankful for how fortunate we had been and wondered what would happen when Mom and Dad saw my clothes. We were especially fearful of how our father would react.

Dad was a factory worker who dropped out of school in the 9th grade to help bring in money for his parents. Because of this, and later, the Depression, he developed an attitude of pinching every penny he made to get the most out of it. His lack of further education had also limited his wage earnings. So, he worked long hours for everything he brought home to his family, from new sleds to winter coats.

As we came nearer to home, we were trying to decide what to tell Mom and Dad about our day, especially the coat. We thought that he would be angry, and were worried about what our punishment might be. Should we lie? Should we say the Vincennes Gang attacked us (There was no gang of boys in a small village of about thirty people!), or some other far-fetched tale? But my brother, who did not have a torn coat, said we should tell the truth.

We went inside the enclosed back porch, and dropped our snowy boots and coats on the floor. Then we entered the back door into the warm kitchen. Mom was at the oven, getting ready to serve the evening meal. Dad was in the bathroom at the front of the house, washing up for supper. We hurriedly told Mom what had happened to the coat and finished just as Dad entered the room.

As I heard Mom retell our story, I braced for what I thought would come. Dad looked at each of us, a frown on his face. I thought he would explode!! Instead, he slowly said that coats could be replaced but his sons could not. I always knew my Dad loved me, but it wasn't until this moment that I realized how deep that love was. He valued us much more than any earthly possession, knowing where the true treasures of life were.

After that day I would like to say that I always was careful not to cause my Dad any problems, money or otherwise. But, being a self-centered, forgetful person, I can't say that happened.

Our Heavenly Father also loves us. But His love is greater than any earthly father's. He can see all the sin I have committed, all the sin I will commit, how often I will turn from Him, or hurt Him. And yet He sent His Son to die for me. I need to remember this daily, ask the Lord for forgiveness, and consistently strive to do His will.

(Written by Perry Parson)
==

 He has said, 'I will never leave you nor forsake you."
Hebrews 13: 5

If you then, being evil, know how to give good gifts to your children, how much more will your Father who is in heaven give what is good to those who ask Him!
Matthew 7: 11

As a father shows compassion to his children, so the Lord shows compassion to those who fear Him.
Psalm 103:13

Meanderings: What is your relationship with your father? Some people respond with: fear, loathing, hate, confusion, anger. Many of those people also have problems with their relationship to the Heavenly Father. Some people respond with: love, respect, honor, joy. Many of those people have a positive relationship with their Heavenly Father. Why is this? How can you improve your relationship with both your earthly Father and your Heavenly Father?

Father, I was blessed with a great dad. He disciplined, celebrated, laughed, explained, encouraged, and loved us. That truly set the stage for my relationship with You. I know that not all people have this positive experience with their fathers. Please help me to be understanding and compassionate to those struggling with the relationships. Help me find the words to lead them to more positive views of both You and their earthly father.

To God be the glory

78. Anxiety

I have never thought of myself as an anxious person. I worried over many situations, but anxiety? No, that was not in my resume. However...

We recently returned home from a wonderful trip to Wales, Ireland and Scotland. Getting there was not a problem. Everything went well at every step. It was the coming home that started giving me flutters.

It began with our early wake up the day we were to leave. I'm not an early morning person. In fact, I'm not a morning person at all. Just let me get up slowly, have some coffee, make no conversation... And no one gets hurt.

I had some anxiety when we went to bed that night that the alarm would not go off... that we had set it for PM instead of AM... that we would not hear it. Of course, with my cochlear implant off at night, I definitely would not hear it, but I counted on Perry hearing it.

No problem. The alarm went off on time. We staggered up, got ready, had breakfast and met our transportation to the Edinburgh airport. The ride through the city and lovely countryside was calm.

Edinburgh airport is really nice, with equally nice people. Even the guy who spotted the jelly in my carry-on luggage was cheerful about it. He held it up with a twinkle in his eyes, shook his finger in a "no no" manner, and bagged my jelly in a little plastic container. Even though I forgot to remove my laptop from the carry-on, they handled it with a smile.   And we all laughed. My last view of the airport was a sign that said, "Haste ye back." No anxiety there! And we didn't even have to take off our shoes!

Then we flew to Munich. I was afraid… a little anxiety… that we would have to go through customs and inspections and all that since we flew in from a foreign country, but no. It was just on to the gate and we were set. Munich didn't even have us put anything through security. Is there an agreement among the European nations? A bit of a problem was that very few things were written in English at the German airport. Usually English is a second language in most European places, but not here. We had to guess at some things and ask for help. We got lost. But they were willing to help. At any rate, it went well. We had been late flying in from Edinburgh; however, they held the plane. We were the last ones on.

But I must admit that at times while wandering in that airport that my heart started to beat a little harder. Lost! Not understanding the language! Late! Anxiety was creeping in.

During the flight to Munich, a Bible verse began playing in my head: *Be anxious for nothing.* At each step with my questions and worries, that verse just kept coming back. *Be anxious for nothing.* Let God know your request. And so we found our way onto the plane, even if we were the last ones.

I had growing anxiety about the next stage of the journey home. That flight was going to be nine hours. Nine hours in an itty bitty seat. But the flight from Munich to Chicago was a little different. First we were in a three seat row. But no one sat beside us. They told us that the plane was absolutely full. Every seat was filled except the one in our row. What that meant was that once in the air, we could put up the armrests, and I could curl up and sleep. Yes! I slept for part of it, allowing me to be more refreshed. God met my need!

We flew on a German airline, which we had never been on before. The seat were a little more spacious and comfy. The hot dinner served to us was really good and they used real flatware. But they didn't pass out snacks or drinks unless you wanted to buy them. To their credit, they did give us a bottle of water, which really was enough. And they gave us one cup of something to drink with the hot meal. On the other hand, the other meal was a disaster. It was a sandwich on soggy brown bread (I suspect it was just defrosted). The sandwich was a slice of cheese, shredded carrots and a piece of zucchini. Yep, that was the whole meal. I'm not a picky eater, but I pulled out the cheese and ate just it. Maybe it's a German thing… maybe a delicious culinary tradition… but folks all over the plane were looking astounded. A guy near us asked the stewardess what it was. She showed astonishment and said, "Why it's a cheese and carrot sandwich!" Anxiety over a cheese sandwich?   No, and I really was not hungry anyway.

We landed in Chicago and it was stormy. We had to sit on the tarmac waiting for a gate to open, and for the storm to pass. I think most of the storm was actually outside the airport, but the sky did look dark and strange. *Be anxious for nothing…* nothing… not even weather. And we escaped the storm.

Chicago O'Hare was the worst airport on the entire trip. Hands down. It was as if none of the airport workers got the same memo. Our boarding pass had no gate listed on it. How difficult could it be to get someone to tell us what gate to use? Apparently very difficult. Anxiety.

We had boarding passes printed out in Edinburgh for the entire trip. And it was no problem using them except for O'Hare. One official told us that we had to get a boarding pass. We showed him or passes. He said those weren't boarding passes, and told us to go to a machine and print out our passes. So we went to the machine, shaking our heads. One guy was behind the machines, and when we said we were having trouble printing the boarding passes, he just shrugged his shoulders and said he couldn't help us. Anxiety.

We had to take moving stairs, elevators, go up and down various floors many times (because the people we asked all gave us different and wrong directions). Finally one guy told us to just go outside on the street, and come in another door. Surprisingly that worked!   Once again, every step of the way, *Be anxious for nothing* kept playing in my mind.

We had to go thru Customs, thru Immigration, thru Passport Control, thru Security Inspection. None of that was too much of a problem. It was finding the gate that was the problem! And because our flight was late into O'Hare, we were also pressed on time to complete all of this and meet our next flight. *Be anxious for nothing.*

But we made it. And our flight from Chicago to DSM went OK, except for the storm that tossed our plane around like a juggler tossing balls. We were sitting just behind the wing, and could see the rain pounding on it. The fascinating thing was watching the rain "explode" around the lights on the wing. It was like green and red fireworks sparking off in every direction. It kept me entertained, which was good because I was quickly losing steam. I just wanted to fall over and sleep, and that was not possible.

We landed in DSM at around 11:30 pm central time, and then a different problem emerged. We had a park/sleep/

fly contract with Ramada, and we have used them before. Basically we leave our car on their lot, they provide the shuttle to and from the airport, and if we need a room, then we stay. This time we did not need a room at the beginning of the trip, but did need one at the end of the trip since we would be arriving so late. So we called the Inn after we collected our baggage, and he came to pick us up. But he mentioned on the ride to the Inn, that there were no available rooms, so he hoped we had a reservation. We told him that we did.

Surprise. When we went to check in, we were that we did NOT have a reservation. And that there were no rooms at any other national chain motel in the area because of a huge convention in town. Well... great. Anxiety raised its ugly head again.

At that point I was ready to sleep in a chair in the lobby. Both of us were having problems thinking straight and even talking straight due to lack of sleep. We pulled up the contract on our phone, and they apologized, saying the worker who checked in our car at the beginning did not put down that we were staying when we returned. Anxiety.

But the clerk said that someone who had a reservation had not yet come. He called that someone and Mr. Someone said he was not going to make it to the motel. So, long story short, we got his room. We got our stuff to the room. Hit the bed. We were immediately asleep!

In a way that I still do not understand, I had peace about that journey, despite the many worrisome situations. Anxiety threatened to cripple me, but God's Word kept me going, even when I didn't know where I was going. Anxiety, then His peace. Anxiety, then His peace. Over and over. His promise was sure, even when I was unsure.

==

Be anxious for nothing, but in everything by prayer and supplication, with thanksgiving, let your requests be made known to God; and the peace of God, which surpasses all understanding, will guard your hearts and minds through Christ Jesus.
Philippians 4:6-7

Can any one of you by worrying add a single hour to your life?
Matthew 6:27

When anxiety was great within me, Your consolation brought me joy.
Psalm 94: 19

Anxiety weighs down the heart, but a kind word cheers it up.
Proverbs 12:25

Meanderings: Anxiety cripples. Are there situations, things, or people who make you anxious? What are the tell-tale signs that anxiety is building in you? Do you have Scriptures that you use to combat anxiety?

Father, I give my anxiety to You over and over, but still I seem to keep inviting it to be a part of my life. I worry too much about things that I cannot change. I fret over timetables, late people, and insecure decisions. I want to be free. To have Your freedom from too much concern. Please clear my mind, help me breathe, help me focus on You and not so much on me. Help me recall Scripture during those times of stress. Thank You for the power You have to break the chains of anxiety.

To God be the glory

79. Don't Pack Your Soul in a Ragged Portfolio

The poet in me beats against my chest and begs to be released. Tonight, as I wander through our deserted little town after dark, I may unleash my errant poet and allow him to frolic as he will. When he has grasped the pen and sketched his soul on paper, I will sigh and take him home. The poet's soul is not easily tamed and he insists on seeing the world through fragments of rose colored glass.

Once upon a time, the poet walked about in daylight, nodding pleasantly to others and presenting himself to all. But there were those who scoffed at the poet, called him a fool, and said that he was too sensitive, too sentimental, too out of touch with the real things.

The poet's lips quivered and tears gathered in his eyes. Without saying a word, he packaged his soul in a ragged portfolio and crept inside the body that housed him. Now he comes out only by coaxing or sometimes by himself, cautiously, when others are not present.

The poet walks on rainbows and skips over dewy hills. The poet laughs and sings and breathes deeply of revitalizing air. The poet smiles at no one in particular and chuckles at himself. The poet steps into nature and rejoices with God.

The poet sees suffering and anguish and pleading eyes. The poet sees kindred souls that are unhappy, confused, bewildered. He becomes sad and silent as the truth of a degraded world and charity-deprived beings slowly sink into his consciousness. Then the poet lifts his eyes... soft gentle eyes... and a sad shy smile to the heavens to ask patience and mercy.

And the poet steps back inside to wait, to wait, to wait...

(Published in *School and Community*, January 1974)

==

 God's voice thunders in marvelous ways; He does great things beyond our understanding. He says to the snow, 'Fall on the earth,' and to the rain shower, 'Be a mighty downpour.'
Job 37:5-6

You have searched me, LORD, and You know me. You know when I sit and when I rise; You perceive my thoughts from afar.
Psalm 139:1

But my God shall supply all your need according to His riches in glory by Christ Jesus.
Philippians 4: 19.

Meanderings: Are there times when you forget who you are? Are you the poet, or the realist? Is it possible to be both, but at different times? Be assured that God is not confused. He created you, He searches you, He knows you. He even knows your thoughts. Perhaps sometimes you are the snow... being gentle in falling to earth with the goal of giving moisture. Perhaps other times you are the mighty downpour, giving moisture with force.

Father, Thank You for creating me so exquisitely that I can be who You want me to be... when You want me in a particular role. Help me listen for Your guidance for when to be gentle or more powerful in my speech. Help me understand the need to be a realist in some situations and a poet in others. Remind me that You are in charge, and that You will use me if I am willing to be used.

To God be the glory

80. Somehow, Someway

Wednesday we went to the library. We: that was my first hour speech class and me, fledgling teacher. They were doing research for panel discussion topics; I was trying to grade week-old papers and answering 5000 questions per minute. Mrs. Wright, the twittering librarian, mother-birded us all.

First hour class was small: about 20 pink and brown blobs that shivered in the wind, quivered in the class, spoke, passed notes, chewed gum, wore ball point tattoos under shirt sleeves, drove cars with fur in the back window, made goo goo eyes at the next table, and in general got their work done somehow, someway. I took a quick eye check around the library.

Paula and her group poured over the books industriously at the far table. Paula: quiet, unassuming, shy, brilliant. She protested in a gentle, embarrassed way when I named her as chairman of her discussion group.

"Please, Miss, I can't do it. I just can't," she pleaded to make her a lesser member. Now she was smiling at Robert, and pointing out a footnote to Bonnie, and writing out the introduction. My eyes wandered on.

Greg came up and nudged my elbow, sending a big check mark across the paper I was grading.

"Gee, I'm sorry," said this half man, half boy, "but if I wanted to find something about making slum places better, where do I look?" I sent him to U for urban renewal, and concentrated on Mark's table.

Mark was new this year, with hair that tickled his nose, and bright acne that came and went without warning. Despite all this, he had a puppy dog smile and worked his tail off. Now he was feverishly turning pages in a magazine, and expounding on police brutality.

"I tell you," he had a voice that someday would be quite commanding. "Civil rights is the thing. We gotta find laws that protect people!"

Pat interrupted. What a contrast: Pat and Mark. Mark... short, excitable, almost spastic in movement and voice. Pat... a transfer from New Orleans, tall, lanky, lazy, who drawled 'Yes mams' and 'No mams'. Who was ecstatic over the first snow.

"Mark," Pat's words were soft as honeysuckle. "I talked to my uncle; he's a policeman, chief, and says only 'bout two percent of all police are really cruel. Just two percent."

MaryAnn had been gazing at Pat's well formed jaw. "Just two percent?"

"Yes, mam. And my uncle, he says...."

Greg bounced by again, sending another ink mark across the paper.

"Gee, I'm sorry." He made an awkward movement of apology, sending the pen flying again. He turned red. "I mean, well, if I want to find out about parks and stuff, like Central Park, where do I look?"

I directed him (hopefully) to R for recreation, and looked towards Mike's table. Mike sacked groceries every night until 10:00 and had six younger brothers and sisters. Maybe that explained why he was always slumped in his seat, and had to push each word out of his mouth with effort. Maybe it was thyroid. Maybe he was susceptible to heart failure. Whatever, Mike was never overheated, and he now slouched, listening to Kevin explain his experiences with UFOs.

"I tell ya, man, they come up out of the reservoir right behind our house. They start in the spring and we see 'em all summer." Somehow, Kevin could grin while keeping up a constant stream of chatter.

"Cool your pipes, Kev," said Mike. "You're just seeing the Christmas lights on the grain elevator."

"In July?" Kevin banged his fist on the table. Even Mike felt the table shake. "I tell ya, man, them's UFOs!"

Greg came close to my table, but not too close. "If I want to find out about traffic problems, where do I look?" I directed him to T for traffic.

Kevin was waving his hand. "Miss, so you believe in UFOs?

I assured him that I thought it was possible.

"Well, then, you can come out and watch 'em come out of the reservoir. The rest of these monkeys can stay here and eat their statistics."

I moved on to Mark's table and asked them if they found enough information. Mark looked up, and scratched his chin. It was getting redder. "I don't know. I just don't know." He returned to his magazine.

"Yes, mam." That was Pat, books shut, ready to go. MaryAnn continued to find his jaw fascinating.

I went to Paula's table. She smiled and said, yes, they had plenty of information.

Mara came by. Poor Mara. After nine weeks of speech, she still moved like a windmill in front of the class, and said everything was "lovely" because she was too nervous to think of another adjective. Greg was pushing her.

"If we want to know about schools in the ghetto, do we look under E for education? That's what Mara said."

I smiled at both of them. They were finally getting it. I rounded the tables, leaving the week-old ungraded papers, dodging Greg, hearing snatches of opinions tempered with research.

"Two percent of police? Baloney! It says here..."
"Honest. Cross my heart. They float out of the reservoir."
"...grain elevator..."
"E... e, d.... Edu...c...ca...educa..."
"Yes, mam, that's what my uncle says...."

Twenty blobs? Is that what I said? Pink and brown? Somehow Wednesday morning, faces were chiseled and profiles sculptured. The bell rang, and I watched my students rise, stretch (except Mike), and leave the library for new conquests. Mara walked by, waving.

Interesting, that first hour. Somehow... someway...

===

 An intelligent heart acquires knowledge, and the ear of the wise seeks knowledge.
Proverbs 18:15

*The fear of the Lord is the beginning of wisdom, and the
knowledge of the Holy One is insight.*
Proverbs 9:10

*There is gold and abundance of costly stones, but the lips
of knowledge are a precious jewel.*
Proverbs 20:15

*For the protection of wisdom is like the protection of
money, and the advantage of knowledge is that wisdom
preserves the life of him who has it.*
Ecclesiastes 7:12

*The beginning of wisdom is this: Get wisdom.
Though it cost all you have, get understanding.*
Proverbs 4:7

*Blessed are those who find wisdom,
those who gain understanding.*
Proverbs 3:13

Meanderings: Why is knowledge
without wisdom a potential danger?
How do knowledge, understanding and
wisdom work together to preserve life
and be a blessing? How would you
define knowledge, wisdom and
understanding? How do those words

differ? How does fear of the Lord lead to wisdom? Can you imagine a nation or a world that truly used wisdom in its dealings? What would it be like?

Father, I pray for our world to seek wisdom and understanding. Too many have knowledge only, but have no idea of how to use it. I pray for leaders of both political entities and churches to go beyond knowledge and acquire wisdom. I pray for families and businesses and organizations to pursue wisdom in their dealings with each other. What a difference this would make to our world! And for myself, I pray that the knowledge I obtain lead to wisdom and understanding of Your ways and Your Word.

To God be the glory

81. Green Sin

I talked with my grandson Dylan about sin this morning. It just came up in the conversation, so I took it as a teachable moment. I filled a clear glass tumbler with a small amount of water and said this is a person who hasn't done anything wrong. But then that person tells a teensy little lie. And with that, I put a drop of green food coloring into the glass.

Then I continued: And then that person thinks a mean thought about his sister. Another drop of green food coloring. And then that person took something from the store and didn't pay for it. Another drop of green food coloring. And that person didn't obey his momma and daddy when he was asked to do something. Another drop of food coloring.

I said, "Sin is like the food coloring. It just changes that person and that person can't get it out by himself."

Dylan said, "You mean you can't get that green out of the water?"

"That's right," I replied. I am just a human, and I can't do it. The only one who can take away sin is God."

Silence as he stared at the glass, now quite dark with green.

"And that's only four drops........" he said.

(Dedicated to Dylan Parson)

===

Or do you not know that wrongdoers will not inherit the kingdom of God? Do not be deceived: Neither the sexually immoral nor idolaters nor adulterers nor men who have sex with men nor thieves nor the greedy nor drunkards nor slanderers nor swindlers will inherit the kingdom of God.
1 Corinthians 6:9-10

If we confess our sins, He is faithful and just and will forgive us our sins and purify us from all unrighteousness.
1 John 1:9

For all have sinned and fall short of the glory of God, and all are justified freely by His grace through the redemption that came by Christ Jesus.
Romans 3:23-24

What comes out of a person is what defiles them. For it is from within, out of a person's heart, that evil thoughts come—sexual immorality, theft, murder, adultery, greed, malice, deceit, lewdness, envy, slander, arrogance and

folly. All these evils come from inside and defile a
person.
Mark 7:20-23

Purify me from my sins, and I will be clean; wash me,
and I will be whiter than snow.
Psalm 51:7

Meanderings: Are there big sins and
little sins, or are all sins repulsive to a
holy God? Do you believe that every
human has sinned? What is the answer
to sin? How do you go from green
sin to being whiter than snow? Can
you do this on your own?

Father, I deal with sin daily. I have thoughts that are
not pure, I say words that I regret, I carry grudges and
do not forgive. I fail to treat others as I wish to be
treated. I break Your commandments. I praise You for
providing the remedy for all the sin that I collect! I am
unable to cleanse myself; You cleanse me with the blood
of Jesus! Thank You for giving me the opportunity to
believe in Jesus, and have my sins washed away!

To God be the glory!

82. The Other Day at Elsie's Store

They hang around Elsie's store. If you can get your
mother to send you for milk or bread in the afternoon,
you'll see them there. Around October, they start to sit
in a circle over by the canned food, but when it's nice,
you'll see them on folding chairs and benches out in
front.

They hang around and smoke and tell stories and talk.
You get the milk or bread and wander around the candy
counter trying to decide what to buy with the change,
and when Elsie goes in the back, Harv (that's her
husband) gives this grin-and-a-nod, and the stories
change, and you go over and look at the canned pumpkin
with sudden great interest.

There aren't many places to hang around in Lowton.
Three to be exact: Elsie's store, the school, and the
church. The school is at one end of town, which isn't
saying much because you can see the bell from all over
the place. It only goes to eighth grade and the big kids
ride the bus into Eldon, so no one hangs around there
much, except to play on the swings and slide.

If you go on up Plum Street ("Runs plum through town,"
Jake used to say), you find Elsie's store. Elsie and Harv
live in the back of the store, and the Lowton Post Office
is in one corner.

Elsie, she's big and has a flat nose, and big white teeth, and wears her hair braided and wrapped around her head. She doesn't say much, but we were all scared of her.

Ever see that picture of the old man and his wife standing outing front of these windows, and the old man is holding a pitchfork? Anyway, Elsie don't look a thing like the woman in the picture, except maybe the mouth. But Harv looked like a cross between the man and the pitchfork. He usually doesn't say much, either, unless you get him started. He just grins and scratches and sells most of the candy while Elsie squeezes herself into the Post Office and reads everyone's mail. My mother said so.

Keep going down Plum street and if you make a quick turn to the left, you'll see the church. It's nothing much; even the stained glass is fake. Brother Myers preaches there on the side. I don't know what else he does, but he doesn't live in Lowton. Just about everybody in Lowton goes to that church, or they don't go at all. Elsie goes; Harv doesn't. Jake goes on Easter. Stoney doesn't go much unless Jessie makes him, and you can tell he isn't happy about being there. Hank goes and sleeps. Alice goes all the time and makes sure everyone knows it.

I wish you could see Alice. She lives real close to the church. I don't know how old she is. Her face is always painted pink, and cracked, like someone took a sledge hammer and made a bull's eye. The cracks were orange and her hair was orange and her mouth was red and big. Alice was fat, but not like Elsie. Elsie never jiggled when she walked; she just bulldozed. But Alice would let one roll meet the air and clear it for the next one. Alice gets drunk all the time; I heard Jessie talk about it. And then she goes to the tent meeting outside town and repents. We snuck in one night and saw her roll down the aisle, and wiggle her hands in the air, and shout, "O, Lordy, save me, a sinner!"

Jake was Dutch and lived down the street from Alice. My mom said those two were a disgrace, living that way. He didn't have any hair, but he had fat eyebrows that were snow white, and real twinkly eyes and fat red cheeks. I thought he would make a real good Santa Claus for the church program, but he only went on Easter. My mom said to stay away from him on account of his reputation. I'm not sure what that is, but we kids liked him. Jake would give us things like wooden marbles and talk in Dutch for us.

Hank lived in the last house in town. He was an old railroad man and only had one eye, and a patch where the other one should have been. Every night when it was nice enough, Hank would sit out on Plum Street and sing, not loud, but kinda sweet and misty like. Gave me goosebumps to hear him. He'd play his banjo and sing songs that made me cry, all about angels and golden hair and stuff. My mom said it was a Welsh lullaby. Hank said he learned it when he was just a kid.

Stoney and Jessie live down the street from Hank. Jessie is fun. She laughs a lot and always gives us food and takes us to swimming lessons. Stoney doesn't have any teeth. He has trouble walking and has to use a cane. Lots of times in the evening, Stoney will get out his harmonica and go across the street. He and Hank would make some real pretty music. I loved to sit and listen.

I guess I've wandered away from Elsie's store, but that's who hung out there: Harv, Jake, Hank and Stoney. Alice would come in a lot and just stare at Jake. Whenever Alice came through the door, Elsie would head for the back, and wouldn't come out until Alice left. Even though they both went to the church, Alice sat on one side and Elsie sat on the other. Hank said he saw Elsie spit on Alice one time. I don't know… Hank sleeps a lot.

The other day, my mom sent me to the store to buy some rice, the kind you have to cook for a long time. She gave me a quarter and said to hurry back. Elsie doesn't carry much rice on account that most of the people in Lowton get commodities. But I like any excuse to go to the store.

They were sitting by the canned goods when I got there. Hank had his banjo and Stoney brought his harmonica. The weather was too nippy to be outside, so the men sat inside. Jake was raising his eyebrows, up and down, up and down. He could really sing good, too. They were trying to talk Harv into bringing out his fiddle. He used to play for a lot of dances, but he doesn't play much anymore. Harv grins and scratches a little, and says nah. He didn't think Elsie would like him dragging out the old squawker.

So anyway, Hank and Stoney are playing something that sounds like an easy wind in the trees, and Jake is sort of humming and singing real low, and Harv is tilted back in his chair smoking a pipe, and dropping ashes on the floor and rubbing them with his heel. I'm looking at the rice and trying to decide between the cheapest and or the biggest, knowing full well I'd take the cheapest and then buy some sugar daddies with the change. Elsie was in the back, or maybe she was in the Post Office reading letters.

Pretty soon, Harv said, " Ya hear about Alice?"

I moved toward the soap and lye, which is next to the canned foods. Jake started taking some checkers out of a little leather bag and gave a low chuckle.
"Nope. What's that woman done this time?"

"She done got herself in the hospital."

Jake put a board over the wood bucket and started arranging checkers. "Oh, yeah?"

"Yeah. Got in a fight."

Stoney quit on the harmonica, but Hank just kept his eye closed and picked real soft-like on his banjo. I move closer to the canned goods.

"A fight, eh?" said Stoney. Some strange things happen in Lowton, but we don't get many fights. Jake finished lining up the blacks and started on the reds.

"Sure wish old Milt was still around," Jake said. "That man could sure play checkers. What happened?"

Harv leaned forward and started arranging his own reds. Hank switched tunes: something about a man drowning and his boat sinking.

"'Bout eight… eight thirty last night, I was locking the doors and Elsie was counting at the cash register, when Alice comes puffing up, banging on the door. I knew it was her, could smell her a mile off, so I look over at Elsie. She just shut the cash register and walked to the back. Didn't say a word. I pull the latch and let Alice in."

Hank drifted into a song about a coal miner and his girl. Jake smiled and moved a checker.

"And then?" said Stoney. Harv scratched his lip and moved a red. I began to read asparagus labels.

"She says to me, she says, 'Where's Elsie? Where's that woman of yours, that lowdown, no good, cheatin', lyin'... ' and Elsie comes out of the back. I lived with that woman close on 40 years and never knew that she could move so fast and so soft.

"Elsie comes up and puts her hands on her hips. I tell you: she looked like the rock of Gibraltar. I just move back. Elsie says, 'What do you mean, Alice, by banging into my store at this hour?'

"Alice was crazy drunk, and by the gleam in her eye, I could tell she had been at the tent meeting. 'You're going to hell, Elsie, for lyin' about me, and for ruinin' my reputation. You're gonna burn, Elsie. Liars don't get to Heaven. You're gonna burn.' Alice picked up one of those Flit guns we keep over there for mosquitos and started for Elsie. I sort of backed up, figured I would let the women fix their own fight."

Harv paused and jumped one of Jake's bait blacks. Jake jumped two reds. Hank was opening his eye now and then, but mostly left it closed. He plinked a few strings, but not much noise came out of the banjo. Stoney rubbed his gums, looked at the checker board, and finally went over to the cash register. He put a nickel on

the counter and pulled a Coke from the cooler. Harv
moved a red into dangerous territory.

"Elsie just stands there and says, 'Alice, you want a cup
of coffee?' Alice is doing her best to move in a straight
line towards Elsie. Pretty soon, they're nose to nose.
They're like twin tanks. Alice raises the Flit gun up in
the air and says, "Ya gonna repent, Elsie?' And Elsie, I
wish you could have seen her, boys, says, 'I ain't done
nothing to repent for, Alice.' Ole Alice starts screaming
in Elsie's mouth. "And who was it told Brother Myers
that I warn't fit to be in church? And who was it
spreading rumors about me and...'"

Harv paused and looked at his checker partner. Jake
chuckled and moved a black.

"She raises that gun a little higher and all of a sudden
Elsie moves her fist out and gets Alice right in the jaw.
Alice goes down like a sack, and Elsie turns around and
goes in the back. I'm left there with Alice on the floor,
and her eyes spinning and her mouth's hanging funny, so
I get her to the car and drive her into town. Yes, sir,
dislocated her jaw."

"What did the sheriff say?" asked Stoney.

"No charges. Said Alice probably got what she
deserved. Said Elsie was just defending herself."

Jake laughed, and it grew to a small roar. Harv and Stoney and Jake pounding their knees and the board and one of the checkers hit Hank and he didn't even know it. He was half asleep and singing a few words now and then. Stoney knocked over his Coke.

"Whoo-eee!" he shouted. "Alice and Elsie, eh? I'd a like to have seen that." He laughed again. Harv wiped his cheek with the back of his hand.

"Don't you worry any about Elsie, boys. She ain't gonna burn in hell so long's she got a good right arm."

I looked at the back of the store, and Elsie was standing in the doorway. She wasn't laughing; she wasn't crying. Just… standing there, filling the doorway and watching them laugh and poke each other and pick up checkers.

I put my quarter on the counter, took the big box of rice, and hurried home.

==

 A good name is better than precious ointment, and the day of death than the day of birth.
Ecclesiastes 7:1

To the pure, all things are pure, but to the defiled and unbelieving, nothing is pure; but both their minds and their consciences are defiled.
Titus 1: 15

The name of the righteous is used in blessings,
 but the name of the wicked will rot.
Proverbs 10:7

But the fruit of the Spirit is love, joy, peace, patience,
kindness, goodness, faithfulness, gentleness, self-control;
against such things there is no law.
Galatians 5: 22-23

Meanderings: The narrator of this
story is a child with limited and
partial knowledge, who repeats what he
has heard or been told. Why must one
be careful when speaking about others,
especially negative aspects? How are
good names trashed? Why are rumors
repeated? How do you protect your
good reputation? How easy is it to
lose a good name, and how difficult is
it to restore a good name?

Father, help me guard my thoughts and words so that I do not give fire to rumors, and so that I do not spread information that could topple a good name. Forgive me when I listen to stories that are harmful about others, and do not try to stop the conversation. Help me protect my name and reputation, and exhibit the fruit of the Spirit.

To God be the glory

83. Tears for Rosa

When I sat at the kitchen table, I could see into Rosa Milano's garden. The air was crisp and bright blue on this October day. Frost had not yet destroyed the gardens. Rosa knelt there tending carrots and turnips and gathering the last of the straggling tomatoes.

She was a small woman with a gaunt olive face. She once had a generous ripe-peach mouth, but now it was drawn into a wilting line. Her eyes were like almonds and her thinning brown hair, thickly floured with white, was drawn into a lapsing bun. Her hands moved quickly among the plants, like a sparrow eating.

Eight children, I thought, eight Milano children and a husband who drinks made her older than me, though we were conceived the same year. I looked about my kitchen, and from there into the living room. Everything was comfortable and clean and warm. We had plenty of food. Andy made good grades in school, and Barry made good money at the plant. Life was good and in order. I looked again at Rosa as she spread straw over the ground. Her house was shabby and sagging. They wore once-over clothes and accepted welfare.

Poor Rosa. I could have told her what life would be like when she married Tare Milano, but she was young and words meant nothing. He was known for drinking too much even then.

"I'm getting married, Angela. Next week… to Tare," she told me one day at school, during our sophomore year. Her chin trembled, and frightened tears crowded her eyes. A swallow, a pastel smile, and then, "I'll have my own house and everything. You'll come, won't you?" Her eyes pleaded acceptance.

I shook my head yes, but all that I could think was that Rosa, who always wanted a room of her own, was now getting her own house.

Her wedding was done in best family tradition with a ceremony in the morning and dancing and feasting into the night. Rosa smiled and danced. They toasted her and sang to her, and carried her to her new husband. He was dark and handsome, but something about his eyes and smile troubled me. The next year, Rosa was 17 and could not dance, with the bulk of the child she carried. She never danced again.

I poured cream into a fresh cup of coffee and reached for another cookie. Was she happy? Did she feel cheated? Did she ever want out? We had talked about it once. Andy was just a baby then, but Rosa had five children. Already she had lost fire and color.

"It's funny, Angela," she had confided. "I hated living at home because there were so many of us. I never had a dress that was just mine. And we slept three to a bed. I hated going to school; I just knew what everyone was saying about me. When Tare asked me to marry him, I figured that I could learn to love him. And I swore by all the saints that my children would never be like me."

She had smiled briefly, as she snapped the green beans in her lap. "My mother told me that I was making a big mistake. She told me that I was just like her and would always be just like her. Know what, Angela? She was right. I didn't have as many children as she did, but life is just the same. I even married an Italian. I didn't escape. Next thing you know, my Jaye Beth will want to marry. It just goes on and on."

We had snapped more beans in silence before she spoke again. "Don't get me wrong, Angela. I love Tare. He is my world. I didn't fall in love with him; I grew in love."

She blotted the corner of her eyes with a handkerchief. "Sure, he had his faults, but he has given me children. A good family is life, itself. I may never buy them new clothes, and only my baby will ever be able to sleep in a bed by herself, but it doesn't matter, not really. I'll do anything for them."

Rosa was generous to a fault. She gave what money she could find to her out-of-work, out-of-school oldest sons so that they could loaf around some wrecked cars. She worked so that she could give money to her husband, who would immediately head to the bar. She had never had much, and would never have much as long as she supported their habits. The only time they would appreciate Rosa would be when she was safely in the ground.

A shiny Buick nosed slowly down the dirt road and stopped in front of Milano's. I moved into the living room to see the driver better. Rather unusual to see a fancy car like that in our little town. A man slid out of the front seat, looked to the left and to the right, and then went to the front door and knocked. When there was no answer, he walked around to the side yard. I returned to the kitchen and peered at the man and Rosa through the window. He had opened the gate and was kneeling by Rosa in the garden. He put his arm around her and together they went into the house. It was much later when he left.

Could it be? Thoughts crowded my head: that man, Rosa... no, of course not, still... I see it every afternoon on television, but it just doesn't happen in the afternoon here. Besides, Rosa was religious. She took all the children to church even though Tare did not attend. But that man? Did Rosa dream, as we all did from time to time? Was she seeking something new?

All the time the man was at Rosa's house, I kept trying to place him. His face was familiar, yet the name would not come to mind. Sometime later, as I made a fresh pot of coffee, I remembered his name. Hinman. Arlie Hinman. He was the superintendent at the mines. I had met him one time at the store. My friend said he lived in another town, but sometimes came into the store for coffee or cream. I thought he was handsome in a Valentino sort of way. I wondered if Rosa thought so, too.

His job must be very handy for him and Rosa, I thought. All he had to do was check for when Tare was working and then drive over to see her. Being a boss like he was, he could probably arrange it just about any time he wanted. How did they meet? Had he come here before? I could not remember him being around. What did he see in her? I tried to shake my thoughts back to the coffee.

Hinman left so late that I could still see his Buick leaving town as the children came home from school. They certainly took a chance on time, I thought.

Andy walked home with the Milano children. I gave him some milk and cookies and drank a cup of coffee. What did Rosa give her children when they came home? And would they notice that her hair was mussed?

Andy went outside to play, but came back in almost immediately. "Mom," he said softly and with wonderment, "Sam Milano's daddy just died. They can't play right now."

The events of the afternoon hit me in the conscience and shame colored my face. Prodigal thoughts came home as I recalled Hinman, Rosa, the comforting arm. How could I give apologies for an errant mind? Hinman, Tare, the mines. Of course. I should have known. Not Rosa. My mind was full of tumbling blocks.

I warmed a casserole to take to the Milano's, along with a salad that I had prepared for supper. Already, I had seen neighbors take some food over. Tess brought a cake and Irene walked there with a basket of something.

Jaye Beth answered my knock. Her young face was streaked and blotched. She took my offering silently, and waved me to the bedroom.

Rosa was seated in a rocking chair, although she remained motionless, and faced the window. Her back was towards the door. "Please go away," she said.

"I just wanted to tell you how sorry I am," I began.

"You never liked Tare."

"He was your man, Rosa. What I think is of no importance."

She suddenly arose, turned and embraced me, then sat down just as quickly. Her eyes were dry, and her face emotionless. She looked as if she had just awakened from an afternoon nap.

"Angela, I don't know what to do or say," she spoke slowly, groping for words. "Sit down. Maybe if I talk to you, it will be better."

"What happened?"

"A slide. It was just one of those things. Happens all the time. Tare was last in line, and he didn't make it out. They might not even get his body out. Mr. Hinman brought me his jacket and lunch pail. Angela, I don't want them to get his body out."

"Don't think such things. You will know what you want later," I tried to comfort her.

We sounded as stilted as bad movie subtitles. It was never easy for me to comfort someone during death, but Rosa made a hard situation even harder. When most people have someone die, they go all to pieces, and then they get more logical later. They ask you without words, to hug them and tell them that everything will be fine. So you say things and do things, and maybe it doesn't mean much, but everyone feels better. I couldn't find those words to say and things to do. My mind was swirling with guilt from my afternoon thoughts. She just sat in her chair after telling me about the slide and said no more. I wanted to leave.

She held Tare's jacket on her lap and moved her fingers over it as if it was a rosary. It had coal dust on it. The collar was stained and the sleeves frayed. At length her fingers ceased picking, and she looked at me.

"I can't cry. I know that you want me to, but I can't. Maybe never. No… don't say anything. Let me finish."

She ran her fingers down the edge of the jacket, caressing the hem, and pulled an envelope from the jacket pocket. She began rocking and tapping the edge of the envelope against her chin.

Finally she spoke. "Suppose that Barry was killed and his boss came to tell you. And he said all the things the company told him to say, but you couldn't hear him. All you can think about is how your man ate his cereal this morning, and that you didn't kiss him goodby because you were mad at him.

" And suppose that boss gave you some things that Barry carried out the door with him: a lunch pail, a jacket. And you remember that you didn't have any ketchup for his sandwiches today, even though he asked specially, so you look into the pail and see that the sandwiches are gone to the last crumb, anyway.

"And you remember that he asked you to fix the hole in his pocket, so you put your hand in there to feel the ragged edges, and you find an envelope. And you can't hardly see 'cause the tears are blearing your eyes, but you wipe them, and look at the envelope. You see that it says, "To Barry from Leila." So you read the letter, and it's a love letter from a woman you don't even know. And she's saying things a woman shouldn't say to a married man.

"You can feel death pulling your bones and anger makes you breathe hard, and sadness makes you go limp. You feel scared, and you want to see him one more time to ask why, and what was she like, and then you want to slap him back into that coal grave. You think about your children and how you can never let them know, and how your face has to look around them, and of the words you have to mouth.

"You tell your friends to go away, and you say that you don't want them to ever find his body. And then you cry, 'O God in Heaven… Mercy! Have mercy!' Angela, you want to cry but my eyes stay barren."

Tare Milano's funeral was simple. A preacher came and prayed. The children filled a whole pew and a half. Most of the villagers came out of respect for Rosa.

Afterward we filed out to the cemetery behind the church. It was gray and misting, but the occasional drop that fell from a leaf onto Rosa's cheek was the only moisture found there. She walked small and straight to the graveside. There wasn't any coffin, but they put a marker where the grave would have been, and Rosa put some flowers on the ground there.

I walked home with Rosa and the children. None of us spoke. I wriggled uncomfortably inside of me, aching to pour out my guilt, my apologies, wanting to burn my thoughts. Barry… what if it was Barry?

I longed to go back to first snows and first loves when life was clean and simple. I wanted to heal, to cover scars. But as we neared our homes, and I watched our children, I knew that innocence was behind us. Memories, words, hurts of the past would lie as coals in a dying fire. Now all I wanted was tears: tears for Rosa, tears for me.

==

 You, therefore, have no excuse, you who pass judgment on someone else, for at whatever point you judge another, you are condemning

yourself, because you who pass judgment do the same things.
Romans 2:1

Do not judge, or you too will be judged.
Matthew 7:1

Do not judge, and you will not be judged. Do not condemn, and you will not be condemned. Forgive, and you will be forgiven.
Luke 6:37

There is only one Lawgiver and Judge, the One who is able to save and destroy. But you—who are you to judge your neighbor?
James 4:12

Meanderings: Have you ever been judged on your words or actions or situations that you have been in? If so, how did you feel? Have you ever been the one doing the judging? Do you need to make amends? Apologize?

Father, I judge far more than I should. I may not say what I am thinking, but nevertheless, it eats at me. Thank You for forgiving me. Help me to not put my nose in other people's business. Help me to not judge based on appearances. Help me to reach out in compassion, to speak Your Word in kindness, and withhold judgement.

To God be the glory

84. Someone's Den in Spanish Modern

She opened the door and slipped inside ever so carefully as not to wake the baby. Snow, like sequins, glittered in her black hair, but lost its magic by the time the door was shut. She began to unbutton her coat, but, changing her mind, ran lightly to the desk where her husband was working with ruler and protractor, and dropped a grimy, snow covered newspaper wrapped package in front of him. Quickly she leaned to kiss him, then straightened, turned and removed her coat. She shook her hair to remove the last of the snow, and when she faced him, the parcel lay unopened on the floor, and he was blotting moisture from his drawing. She wept.

He tickles me sometimes on my belly or my chin and I say cut-it-out and he laughs and reaches out again and I laugh and cry and run away and come back in an hour or 15 minutes and I don't worry too much about it because it is only today and tomorrow I may do something great or he may be famous and tickle me all day because I won't care then.

Oh, we'll have money then, just hanging from the ceiling and I'll sew bills together to make clothes or loin cloths or baby blankets and I'll buy flowers or demitasse and we'll go on picnics and invite the maid but he said forget it what's wrong with you and tries to plan someone's den in Spanish modern and I pinch him because I'm a dreamer in Barcelona and he pinched me because he is the handsome young violin player in velvet rags.

We used to walk or run to see each other and now we are married and sometimes we are happy or sad but mostly we love each other because I have long hair or he has a beard or we have a baby and we play with the baby or ride bicycles in the Commons or on Beacon Street and come home to boil frankfurters and live together until tomorrow or the next day, whichever comes first, but he said what's wrong with you Julian or Gregory invented the calendar or Stonehenge and the next day is tomorrow and the rent is due, but never mind I said we've always been able to pay it.

Maybe he is a fishmonger and I am a mermaid and we have a baby or mermette but he says no she is just all wet or spilled her milk and do we have more so I check but the box is empty or the heat is off or the faucet drips or two of the above or all the above which means we all go to bed together or use the biggest blanket and I feed the baby and we are happy and warm but very poor I think.

We have one window and take turns looking at the alley except for the baby and she doesn't care about what's outside as long as her mouth is full and we have an ebony statue etched in gold only three inches high that sits on the window sill and looks at the alley or the sky all day and most of the night I suppose and knows

everything there is to know about what goes on, but I
don't envy the statue it was a wedding gift and I don't
want to know everything except why can't he make
some money or support his family or pay the rent but it
doesn't speak only looks at the alley.

He says my problem is that I'm not real so why don't I
go live with my mother she is just like me and quit
bugging him about the rent he knows it's due and soon's
he sells the plan maybe he'll throw the landlord out or
maybe he'll move out forget the landlord so I put on my
coat and say who gets the statue and do you want the
baby or shall I take her is that real enough and he says
he's sorry it's just that money makes him nervous and I
say no money makes me nervous and take off my coat
because I decided to stay awhile to make sure my love
takes care of himself.

Oh, for more snow to cover the alley and make
everything pure or white or innocent again and he says
what's wrong with you we're past that stage and soon's
he sells that plan things won't be so black maybe gray
but never white again so I nibble his ear and tell him he's
a romantic and he growls which makes me remember all
over again my empty stomach and the unfulfilled rent
stub but it starts to snow finally I knew it would and it
was too gray not to and it's beautiful but cold outside
and I'm glad I'm inside but I wonder how long.

We eat soup or bread and gravy or green beans for supper and remember old midnight feasts of boiled eggs and pumpernickel when we burned candles because we liked candles and sang because we liked music but now he say shut up he can't concentrate when I hum and he sketches black and red for someone's den in Spanish Modern while we live gray and black in Early Attic and boil the same bones twice in a row.

Maybe it was a mistake to get married I think about it and put on my coat so he says where are you going but I smile instead of answering and go out into the snowy alley and it's cold but so white there still can be white you see it's all over out there white as far you can see and somewhere in the alley or a back street or an obscure dump someone threw away some flowers mostly dead so what some were still alive I will give him one and he will smell it and remember the old days and laugh again because he knows there is white we will love again because he will finish the plan and pay the rent oh I bless the wilted flower for its magic and wrap it in newspaper to give to him.

The room is so small; one wonders how two fit into it. The walls are sooty, the furniture faded and torn, and a musty smell, an old smell permeates the four walls. A man and a woman: he is bent over a desk; she is kneeling on the floor beside a tiny bit of soggy, ink run newspaper and one wilted flower. And on the desk is a drawing of a stately mansion and drops of water rivulet it, blending blacks and reds and ink lines, and the many little streams streak the house and course through the map, surging the tiny domain, flooding its walls and erasing the architect's last marks.

From somewhere, a baby cries and there is the sound of autos slipping on slushy streets, tenement mothers calling their children, and a lone dog howling for a mate. Lights begin to dot the city as dusk follows the snow in covering it. But no light, no sound comes from the tiny room. Only water cascades through some's den in Spanish modern.

(2nd Place Winner of *Writer's Digest* Short Story Contest, 1978)

==

 Have I not commanded you? Be strong and courageous. Do not be afraid; do not be discouraged, for the LORD your God will be with you wherever you go.
Joshua 1:9

And we know that in all things God works for the good of those who love Him, who have been called according to His purpose.
Romans 8:28

Be strong, and let your heart take courage, all you who wait for the Lord!
Psalm 31:24

Rejoice in hope, be patient in tribulation, be constant in prayer.
Romans 12:12

Love bears all things, believes all things, hopes all things, endures all things.
1 Corinthians 13:17

Meanderings: Discouragement hits all of us. What is something that has discouraged you? How did you overcome this? Which of these verses would you give to the young couple in the story? Why?

Father, when I am discouraged, help me remember to turn to Your Word. Help me remember that You care, and that You provide. Thank You for Your constant faithfulness in my life. Thank You for the promise that You will be with me wherever I go. Forgive me when I forget You.

To God be the glory

About Me

I'm a retired teacher, a wife, mom, grandma, great grandma, sister, daughter, neighbor, and friend. I live a life permeated with joy and peace and happiness and punctuated with fantastic people.

I like to read, write, scrapbook, cook, do yoga, garden, travel, and praise my Lord God. I try to be a good steward of what we have and discover new ways to do things. I chastise myself every so often. I have strong opinions. And I am curious, which sometimes gets me into trouble. I think, and sometimes come to the wrong conclusions. I'm an observer. You might see all these come out in the book.

Most of all, I am a born again believer who firmly believes that every person has a purpose.

To God be the Glory!

Other books by Diana Newquist Parson

Right Here... Right Now... Musings

Right Here... Right Now... Memories

Made in the USA
Las Vegas, NV
21 August 2023

76404299R00164